First World War
and Army of Occupation
War Diary
France, Belgium and Germany

29 DIVISION
86 Infantry Brigade
Royal Dublin Fusiliers
1st Battalion
19 March 1916 - 30 September 1917

WO95/2301/1

The Naval & Military Press Ltd
www.nmarchive.com
Published in association with The National Archives

Published by

The Naval & Military Press Ltd

Unit 10 Ridgewood Industrial Park,

Uckfield, East Sussex,

TN22 5QE England

Tel: +44 (0) 1825 749494

www.naval-military-press.com

www.nmarchive.com

This diary has been reprinted in facsimile from the original. Any imperfections are inevitably reproduced and the quality may fall short of modern type and cartographic standards.

© Crown Copyright
Images reproduced by permission of The National Archives, London, England, 2015.

Contents

Document type	Place/Title	Date From	Date To
Heading	WO95/2301-1 1 Battalion Royal Dublin Fusiliers 1916 Mar-1917 Sept		
Heading	29th Division 86th Infy Bde. 1st Bn Roy. Dub. Fus. Mar 1916-Dec 1917 Sep From U K Serving With 16 Div 48 Bde From 1917 Oct-1918 Apl		
Heading	29th Division. 86th Infantry Brigade. Arrived Marseilles from E.E.F. 19.3.16 1st Battalion Royal Dublin Fusiliers March 1916 Dec 98		
War Diary	France Marseilles	19/03/1916	20/03/1916
War Diary	Aboard Train	20/03/1916	22/03/1916
War Diary	Pont Remy	22/03/1916	22/03/1916
War Diary	Domqueur	23/03/1916	31/03/1916
Miscellaneous	Time Table for Brigade Route March	26/03/1918	26/03/1918
Miscellaneous	Brigadier-General W.L. Williams, D.S.O. Commanding 56th Infantry Brigade.	28/03/1916	28/03/1916
Miscellaneous	Operation Only		
Heading	29th Division. 86th Infantry Brigade. 1st Battalion Royal Dublin Fusiliers April 1916		
War Diary	France Beauval	01/04/1916	04/04/1916
War Diary	Acheux	05/04/1916	11/04/1916
War Diary	France Acheux	12/04/1916	12/04/1916
War Diary	Auchonvillers (Firing Line)	13/04/1916	13/04/1916
War Diary	Auchonvillers	14/04/1916	17/04/1916
War Diary	Auchonvillers (Firing Line)	18/04/1916	22/04/1916
War Diary	Mailly Maillet	23/04/1916	28/04/1916
War Diary	Louvencourt	29/04/1916	01/05/1916
Miscellaneous	Outposts.	01/04/1916	01/04/1916
Miscellaneous	A Form. Messages And Signals.		
Miscellaneous	To 1/Re. D.F.	17/04/1916	17/04/1916
Miscellaneous	C Form. (Duplicate). Messages And Signals.		
Miscellaneous	A Form. Messages And Signals.		
Miscellaneous	A Form. Messages And Signals.	24/04/1916	24/04/1916
Miscellaneous	O/C I.R. Dublin Two	27/04/1916	27/04/1916
Miscellaneous	O/C I Rs F		
Miscellaneous	Staff Captain, 86th Brigade.	21/04/1916	21/04/1916
Miscellaneous	1/Royal Dublin Fus	22/04/1916	22/04/1916
Map	Auchonvillers		
Miscellaneous	1.R. Dublin Fus.	24/04/1916	24/04/1916
Miscellaneous	1.R. Dublin Fus.	28/04/1916	28/04/1916
Miscellaneous	The Adjustment 1st. Royal Dublin Fusiliers.		
Operation(al) Order(s)	Operation Orders No. 1	24/08/1916	24/08/1916
Miscellaneous	O.C. 1st R. Dublin Fusr	29/04/1916	29/04/1916
Miscellaneous	29th Division.	29/04/1916	29/04/1916
Miscellaneous	29th Division. 86th Infantry Brigade. May & June 1916 1st Battalion Royal Dublin Fusiliers May & June 1916		
War Diary	Louvencourt	02/05/1916	08/05/1916
War Diary	Firing Line Near Auchonvillers	09/05/1916	18/05/1916
War Diary	Mailly Mallet	19/05/1916	28/05/1916
War Diary	Louvencourt	29/05/1916	07/06/1916
War Diary	Firing Line Near Auchonvillers	08/06/1916	15/06/1916

Type	Description	Start	End
War Diary	Mailly Wood	16/06/1916	19/06/1916
War Diary	Firing Line (Auchonvillers)	20/06/1916	23/06/1916
War Diary	Acheux	24/06/1916	30/06/1916
Operation(al) Order(s)	Operation Order No. By Capt A.J. Trigona Comdg For Royal Dublin Fusiliers 2nd May 1916	02/05/1916	02/05/1916
Miscellaneous	86th Brigade Exercise	03/05/1916	03/05/1916
Map			
Miscellaneous	To Tau 4 PM		
Miscellaneous	Special Order by Lieut. Col. H. Nelson. D.S.O. Commanding 1/Royal Dublin Fusiliers. Monday, 8th May 1916	08/05/1916	08/05/1916
Miscellaneous	Inspection of Billets.	08/05/1916	08/05/1916
Miscellaneous	Dardanelles	28/06/1915	28/06/1915
Operation(al) Order(s)	Operation Order by Lieut. Col H. Nelson, D.S.O. Commanding 1st Royal Dublin Fusiliers Wednesday 17th May 1916	17/05/1916	17/05/1916
Operation(al) Order(s)	Operation Order by Lieut. Col H. Nelson, D.S.O. Commanding 1st Royal Dublin Fusiliers Thursday 18th May 1916	18/05/1916	18/05/1916
Operation(al) Order(s)	Operation Order by Lieut. Col H. Nelson, D.S.O. Commanding 1st Royal Dublin Fusiliers Saturday 27th May 1916	27/05/1916	27/05/1916
Miscellaneous	86th Brigade Preliminary Operation Order. for training purposes only.	31/05/1916	31/05/1916
Miscellaneous	Orders by Lt. Colonel Nelson, Commanding 1st R.D.F.		
Miscellaneous	H. Qr Coy to O.C. Corp To O.C. Coys		
Operation(al) Order(s)	Operation Order by Lieut. Col. H. Nelson. D.S.O. Commanding 1st Royal Dublin Fusiliers. 5th June 1916	05/06/1916	05/06/1916
Operation(al) Order(s)	Operation Order by Lieut. Col. H. Nelson. D.S.O. Commanding 1st Royal Dublin Fusiliers. 6th June 1916	06/06/1916	06/06/1916
Miscellaneous	1st Royal Dublin Fusiliers.	15/06/1916	15/06/1916
Operation(al) Order(s)	Operation Orders by Lieut. Col. H. Nelson, D.S.O. Commanding 1st Royal Dublin Fusiliers. 17th June 1916	17/06/1916	17/06/1916
Miscellaneous	O.C. 1st Royal Dublin Fus	17/06/1916	17/06/1916
Operation(al) Order(s)	Order For The Move.	18/06/1916	18/06/1916
Miscellaneous	O.C. 1st Bn. R. Dunlin Fusiliers.	19/06/1916	19/06/1916
Miscellaneous	Order For The Move, by Lieut. Col. H. Nelson, D.S.O. Commanding 1st Royal Dublin Fusiliers, Thursday 22nd June, 1916. In the Field.	22/06/1916	22/06/1916
Miscellaneous	After Order by Lieut. Col. H. Nelson, D.S.O. Commanding 1st Royal Dublin Fusiliers, Tuesday 20th June, 1916. In the Field.	20/06/1916	20/06/1916
Miscellaneous	B.M.A. 4. 23/6/16	23/06/1916	23/06/1916
Operation(al) Order(s)	Operation Orders by Lieut. Col. H. Nelson, D.S.O. Commanding 1st Royal Dublin Fusiliers.	26/06/1918	26/06/1918
Miscellaneous	Appendix A.		
Map	Secret		
Map			
Miscellaneous	G 46 13th June 1916	13/06/1916	13/06/1916
Heading	29th Division. 86th Infantry Brigade. 1st Battalion Royal Dublin Fusiliers July 1916		
Heading	War Diary of 1st Bn Royal Dublin Fusiliers for July 1916		
War Diary	Firing Line (Auchonvillers)	01/07/1916	04/07/1916
War Diary	Mailly Wood	05/07/1916	15/07/1916

War Diary	Firing Line (Mesnil)	16/07/1916	23/07/1916
War Diary	Warnimont Wd	24/07/1916	24/07/1916
War Diary	Beauval	25/07/1916	27/07/1916
War Diary	Wormhoudt	28/07/1916	31/07/1916
Operation(al) Order(s)	Orders For The Move by Lieut. Col. H. Nelson, D.S.O. Commanding 1st Royal Dublin Fusiliers, 14th July, 1916 In the Field.	14/07/1916	14/07/1916
Heading	29th Division. 86th Infantry Brigade. 1st Battalion Royal Dublin Fusiliers. August 1916		
Heading	War Diary of 1st Battn Royal Dublin Fusiliers From 1st August 1916 To 31st August 1916 Volume		
War Diary	Poperinghe (Camp 'J')	01/08/1916	03/08/1916
War Diary	Camp 'O'	04/08/1916	08/08/1916
War Diary	Canal Bank Ypres	09/08/1916	09/08/1916
War Diary	Firing Line (Wieltje)	10/08/1916	10/08/1916
War Diary	Firing Line	11/08/1916	19/08/1916
War Diary	Convent Ypres	20/08/1916	29/08/1916
War Diary	Camp 'O'	30/08/1916	30/08/1916
Heading	29th Division. 86th Infantry Brigade. 1st Battalion Royal Dublin Fusiliers September 1916		
Heading	War Diary of 1st Bn Royal Dublin Fusiliers. From 1st September to 30th September 1916 Volume		
War Diary	Camp 'O'	01/09/1916	08/09/1916
War Diary	Canal Bank Ypres	09/09/1916	09/09/1916
War Diary	Firing Line St Jean	10/09/1916	14/09/1916
War Diary	Firing Line	14/09/1916	14/09/1916
War Diary	Canal Bank	15/09/1916	18/09/1916
War Diary	Firing Line Potisze	19/09/1916	23/09/1916
War Diary	Convent Ypres	24/09/1916	28/09/1916
War Diary	Camp 'C'	29/09/1916	29/09/1916
War Diary	Camp 'O'	30/09/1916	30/09/1916
Heading	29th Division 86th Infantry Brigade. 1st Battalion Royal Dublin Fusiliers October 1916		
Heading	War Diary of 1st Battn Royal Dublin Fusiliers From 1st October 1916 To 31st October 1916 Volume 22		
War Diary	Camp 'O'	01/10/1916	01/10/1916
War Diary	(Nr Poperinghe)	02/10/1916	04/10/1916
War Diary	Wormhoudt	05/10/1916	08/10/1916
War Diary	La Neuville (Nr. Corbie)	09/10/1916	10/10/1916
War Diary	Dernancourt	11/10/1916	13/10/1916
War Diary	Mametz Wood	14/10/1916	19/10/1916
War Diary	Firing Line Flers	20/10/1916	23/10/1916
War Diary	Delville Wd	24/10/1916	25/10/1916
War Diary	Firing Line Flers	26/10/1916	27/10/1916
War Diary	Delville Wood	28/10/1916	29/10/1916
War Diary	Mametz Wood	30/10/1916	30/10/1916
War Diary	Ville-Sous-Corbie	31/10/1916	31/10/1916
Heading	29th Division 86th Infantry Brigade. 1st Battalion Royal Dublin Fusiliers November 1916		
Heading	War Diary of 1st Battn Royal Dublin Fusiliers From 1st to 30th November 1916 Volume		
War Diary	Corbie	01/11/1916	16/11/1916
War Diary	Meaulte	17/11/1916	18/11/1916
War Diary	Carnoy Camp	14/11/1916	21/11/1916
War Diary	Bernafay Camp	22/11/1916	24/11/1916
War Diary	Firing Line (Les Boeufs)	25/11/1916	26/11/1916

War Diary	Firing Line	27/11/1916	27/11/1916
War Diary	Carnoy Camp	28/11/1916	30/11/1916
Heading	29th Division. 86th Infantry Brigade. 1st Battalion Royal Dublin Fusiliers December 1916		
Heading	War Diary of 1st Royal Dublin Fusiliers from 1.12.16 to 31.12.16 Vol 9		
War Diary	Carnoy	01/12/1916	01/12/1916
War Diary	Bernafay Camp	02/12/1916	03/12/1916
War Diary	Firing Line Les Boeufs	04/12/1916	06/12/1916
War Diary	Bernafay Camp	07/12/1916	07/12/1916
War Diary	Carnoy Camp	08/12/1916	11/12/1916
War Diary	Meaulte	12/12/1916	13/12/1916
War Diary	Conde	14/12/1916	14/12/1916
War Diary	Saisseval	15/12/1916	31/12/1916
Heading	War Diary of 1st Battn Royal Dublin Fusiliers From 1st January 1917 To 31st January 1917 Volume 23		
War Diary	Saisseval	01/01/1917	09/01/1917
War Diary	Quesnoy	10/01/1917	10/01/1917
War Diary	Corbie	11/01/1917	11/01/1917
War Diary	Meaulte	12/01/1917	12/01/1917
War Diary	Carnoy	13/01/1917	13/01/1917
War Diary	Guillemont	14/01/1917	14/01/1917
War Diary	Trenches Morval Sector	15/01/1917	16/01/1917
War Diary	Carnoy	17/01/1917	19/01/1917
War Diary	Guillemont	20/01/1917	20/01/1917
War Diary	Firing Line	21/01/1917	22/01/1917
War Diary	Carnoy	23/01/1917	25/01/1917
War Diary	Guillemont	26/01/1917	26/01/1917
War Diary	Firing Line Morval Sector	27/01/1917	28/01/1917
War Diary	Carnoy	29/01/1917	31/01/1917
Heading	War Diary of the 1st Bn. Royal Dublin Fusiliers. From 1st February 1917 To 28th February 1917 Volume 26		
War Diary	Guillemont	01/02/1917	01/02/1917
War Diary	Firing Line Morval Sector	02/02/1917	03/02/1917
War Diary	Carnoy	04/02/1917	06/02/1917
War Diary	Meaulte	07/02/1917	07/02/1917
War Diary	Laneuville	08/02/1917	18/02/1917
War Diary	Meaulte	19/02/1917	19/02/1917
War Diary	Maltz Horn	20/02/1917	20/02/1917
War Diary	Bouleau Wood	21/02/1917	21/02/1917
War Diary	Firing Line	22/02/1917	23/02/1917
War Diary	Hardecourt	24/02/1917	24/02/1917
War Diary	Bronfay Camp	25/02/1917	26/02/1917
War Diary	Hardecourt Camp	27/02/1917	27/02/1917
War Diary	Front Line	28/02/1917	28/02/1917
Miscellaneous	Appendix A Report on Operations 28th February/1st March 1917	28/02/1917	28/02/1917
Heading	War Diary of 1st Royal Dublin Fusiliers From 1st March 1917 To 31 March 1917 Volume No 27		
War Diary	Front Line	01/03/1917	01/03/1917
War Diary	Hardecourt	02/03/1917	02/03/1917
War Diary	Bronfay Camp	03/03/1917	03/03/1917
War Diary	Ville Sur Corbie	04/03/1917	07/03/1917
War Diary	Ville	08/03/1917	20/03/1917
War Diary	Mericourt	21/03/1917	22/03/1917
War Diary	Belloy	23/03/1917	29/03/1917

War Diary	Soues	30/03/1917	30/03/1917
War Diary	Halloy	31/03/1917	31/03/1917
Heading	War Diary 1st Royal Dublin Fusrs For The Month Of April 1917 Volume 26		
War Diary	Halloy Les Pernois	01/04/1917	01/04/1917
War Diary	Longuevillette	02/04/1917	02/04/1917
War Diary	Beaurepaire	03/04/1917	04/04/1917
War Diary	Beaudricourt.	05/04/1917	07/04/1917
War Diary	Bavincourt	08/04/1917	09/04/1917
War Diary	Simoncourt	11/04/1917	11/04/1917
War Diary	Arras	12/04/1917	14/04/1917
War Diary	Orange Hill	15/04/1917	17/04/1917
War Diary	Firing Line. Monchy	18/04/1917	21/04/1917
War Diary	Arras	22/04/1917	22/04/1917
War Diary	Orange Hill	23/04/1917	23/04/1917
War Diary	Firing Line Monchy	24/04/1917	24/04/1917
War Diary	Arras	25/04/1917	25/04/1917
War Diary	Wanquetin	26/04/1917	26/04/1917
War Diary	Souastre	27/04/1917	30/04/1917
Heading	War Diary 1st Royal Dublin Fusiliers May, 1917 (Volume XXVII)		
War Diary	Gouy-En-Artois	01/05/1917	01/05/1917
War Diary	Arras	02/05/1917	10/05/1917
War Diary	Berneville	11/05/1917	14/05/1917
War Diary	Arras	15/05/1917	20/05/1917
War Diary	Brown Line	21/05/1917	23/05/1917
War Diary	Monchy	24/05/1917	31/05/1917
Heading	1st Bn, Royal Dublin Fusiliers. War Diary for month of June 1917. Volume No, 27		
War Diary	Arras	01/06/1917	01/06/1917
War Diary	Berneville	02/06/1917	02/06/1917
War Diary	Pernois	03/06/1917	27/06/1917
War Diary	Penois	27/06/1917	27/06/1917
War Diary	Proven aras	28/06/1917	30/06/1917
Heading	War Diary of 1st Royal Dublin Fusiliers For Month of July 1917 Volume 28 Vol 16		
War Diary	Proven area	01/07/1917	04/07/1917
War Diary	Belgium 28. N.W. 1/20000 Edition S.A. A.10.d In a Wood	05/07/1917	12/07/1917
War Diary	Canal Bank B.24 b. 9.6 (Belgium Sheet 28 N.W.)	13/07/1917	13/07/1917
War Diary	Canal Bank B 24. b 9.6 (Belgium 28 N.W.) (Bat. Hdqts)	13/07/1917	17/07/1917
War Diary	Canal Bank B 24 b 9.6 (Belgium Sheet 2 8 NW) Batt HQ	18/07/1917	19/07/1917
War Diary	Camp Crombeke Poperinge Road	20/07/1917	24/07/1917
War Diary	Camp Provenarea No 3	25/07/1917	30/07/1917
War Diary	Proven Area No. 3	30/07/1917	30/07/1917
War Diary	Proven Area No. 2	31/07/1917	31/07/1917
Heading	War Diary of 1st Bn Royal Dublin Trenches For Month Of August 1917 Volume 29 Vol 17		
War Diary	Proven Area No. 2 Belgium Sheet 9 X20d 5.3	01/08/1917	03/08/1917
War Diary	Forrest Area Camp 13	04/08/1917	05/08/1917
War Diary	Camp 1200x Of Woesten	06/08/1917	06/08/1917
War Diary	Camp B.7.C.	06/08/1917	06/08/1917
War Diary	Saules Fm	07/08/1917	07/08/1917
War Diary	Captains Fm.	08/08/1917	09/08/1917

War Diary	B.7.C (Belgium Sheet 28 N.W.)	10/08/1917	10/08/1917
War Diary	Dewippe Camp	11/08/1917	14/08/1917
War Diary	Eton Camp B.7.C	15/08/1917	15/08/1917
War Diary	Cannes Fm W 22 A. 2.2 Broembeek Edit 1/10000	16/08/1917	17/08/1917
War Diary	Cannes Fm	18/08/1917	20/08/1917
War Diary	Bbingly Camp B.7.C. 6.6	21/08/1917	22/08/1917
War Diary	Abbingly Camp	23/08/1917	25/08/1917
War Diary	Charter House. Camp B.9.C	26/08/1917	28/08/1917
War Diary	Petworth Camp X 25d. 4.7 (Belgium 19. SE)	29/08/1917	31/08/1917
Heading	War Diary of 1st Royal Dublin Fusiliers For Month Of September 1917 Volume 30 Vol 18		
War Diary	Petworth Camp X 25d 4.7 (Belgium 19.SE)	01/09/1917	04/09/1917
War Diary	Petworth Camp	04/09/1917	10/09/1917
War Diary	Oxford Camp Near Elverdinghe 28/N.W/B.9.d.88	11/09/1917	14/09/1917
War Diary	Petworth Camp (Proven 3 Area X 25d 47 Belgium 19.SE)	15/09/1917	15/09/1917
War Diary	Petworth Camp	16/09/1917	16/09/1917
War Diary	Herzeele	17/09/1917	19/09/1917
War Diary	Petworth Camp	20/09/1917	21/09/1917
War Diary	Eton Camp (28 N.W. B 7b)	22/09/1917	25/09/1917
War Diary	Eton Camp	26/09/1917	28/09/1917
War Diary	Langemarck U.23.c.1.15	29/09/1917	29/09/1917
War Diary	Eton Camp	30/09/1917	30/09/1917
Heading	1/R Dubs Capt Tarletion October 1917		
Miscellaneous	Captain GWB Tarleton	07/10/1917	07/10/1917
Heading	Lt M F O Donnell 1 R Dubs		
Miscellaneous	A Brief War Record of Lt. M.F. O'Donnell, M.C., 12, Leinster Sq., Rathmines, Dublin.		
Miscellaneous	1st Battalion The Royal Dublin Fusiliers. Memoranda.		

WO 95/2301/1

1 Battalion Royal Dublin Fusiliers

1916 Sept
Mar - 1917 Sept.

29TH DIVISION
86TH INFY BDE.

1ST BN ROY. DUB. FUS.
MAR 1916-DEC 1916
1917 SEP
UK

Serving with 16 Div. 48 BDE
from 1917 OCT – 1918 APL

29th Division.

86th Infantry Brigade.

Arrived Marseilles from E.E.F. 19.3.16.

1st BATTALION

ROYAL DUBLIN FUSILIERS

MARCH 1 9 1 6

Army Form C. 2118.

WAR DIARY
or
INTELLIGENCE SUMMARY.
(Erase heading not required.)

10²ᵈ (1ˢᵗ R.D.F.) March 19ᵗʰ – June 30ᵗʰ 1916.

Instructions regarding War Diaries and Intelligence Summaries are contained in F. S. Regs., Part II. and the Staff Manual respectively. Title pages will be prepared in manuscript.

Place	Date	Hour	Summary of Events and Information	Remarks and references to Appendices
FRANCE				
MARSEILLES	19/3/16		Arrived at MARSEILLES early in morning: disembarked during afternoon & entrained.	
– do –	20/3/16		Left MARSEILLES any early in morning – about 0230 – for unknown destination.	
ON BOARD TRAIN	21/3/16 to 25/3/16		Travelling steadily North through FRANCE by train.	
PONT REMY	26/3/16		Arrived at PONT REMY and detrained during daylight & debussed. Marched to DOMQUEUR where Bn. went into Billets.	
DOMQUEUR	27/3/16 to 29/3/16		Bn. training.	
– do –	30/3/16		Rear "C" J.H. opened.	
– do –	31/3/16		Bn. with remainder of 86 Bde. moved up to BEAUVAL into Billets.	

T2134. Wt. W708-776. 500000. 4/15. Sir J.C. & S.

TIME TABLE
for
BRIGADE ROUTE MARCH

1. The Brigade - as strong as possible - will carry out a Route March on 27th March. Starting Point - the cross roads half mile south of the S of MAISON-ROLLAND.

   Route from starting point - St. RIQUIER - COULONVILLERS - DOMQUEUR (via the YVRENCH - DOMQUEUR road.

2. Dress.   Marching order without packs.

3. 120 S.A.A. will be carried on the soldier.

4. 1st. Line Transport as follows will march brigaded in rear of the column. -

    Per Battalion:-   4 Cooking Carts.
                      2 Water Carts (filled)
                      1 Maltese Cart.
                      1 Officers' Mess Cart.
                      1 Limber.
                      9 Pack Animals.

5. <u>Order of March</u> - Machine Gun Coy.) will pass the
                             1st. R.Dublin Fsrs.)   S.P. at 10 a.m.

    1st. Lancs. Fsrs.
    1st. R. Munster Fsrs.
    2nd. Royal Fusiliers.
    1st. Line Transport in order of march.

6. 1st. Line Transport of Battalions will leave the route to S.P. clear until the troops have passed.

    (Reference Map - AMIENS No. 12.)

Signed
Captain
Staff Captain, 86th Bde.

No. 2.

ADVANCE BRIGADE ORDERS by
Brigadier-General L.L. WILLIAMS, D.S.O.
Commanding 48th Infantry Brigade.
28th March, 1918.

17. PRACTICE MOVE.

The Brigade will practice moving from billets
tomorrow, 29th inst., All men are to leave billets and all
stores are to be taken.

The Royal Fusiliers will move along the road running E
from COULONVILLERS and will halt at 11 a.m. at the junction of
the COULONVILLERS-BEAUMETZ and LONGVILLERS-DOMQUEUR roads near
point 25.

The R. Munster Fusiliers will move along the same road
as the Royal Fusiliers and will halt at 11 a.m. in rear of the
Royal Fusiliers on the COULONVILLERS-BEAUMETZ road.

The R. Dublin Fusiliers will move along the road running
N.E. to LONGVILLERS and will halt at 11 a.m. near point 25
at the junction of the DOMQUEUR-LONGVILLERS and COULONVILLERS-
BEAUMETZ roads.

The Lancashire Fusiliers will move via DOMQUEUR to LONGVILLERS
and will halt at 11 a.m. in rear of the R.Dublin Fusiliers on
the DOMQUEUR-LONGVILLERS road.

Pack animals are to be in rear of companies.

All other transport of the Royal Fusiliers and R.Munster
Fusiliers to be in rear of the R.Munster Fusiliers, and the
transport of the R.Dublin Fusiliers and Lancashire Fusiliers
in rear of the Lancashire Fusiliers.

Billeting Officers will report to the Brigade Major at
LONGVILLERS that all stores have been removed from billets.

29th Division.
86th Infantry Brigade.

1st BATTALION

ROYAL DUBLIN FUSILIERS

APRIL 1916

Army Form C. 2118.

WAR DIARY
or
INTELLIGENCE SUMMARY.
(Erase heading not required.)

Instructions regarding War Diaries and Intelligence Summaries are contained in F.S. Regs., Part II. and the Staff Manual respectively. Title pages will be prepared in manuscript.

Place	Date	Hour	Summary of Events and Information	Remarks and references to Appendices
FRANCE				
BEAUVAL	1/4/16		Bn. Training	
-do-	2/4/16		Day of Rest	
-do-	3/4/16		Bn. Training	
-do-	4/4/16		Bn. moved up to ACHEUX	
ACHEUX	5/4/16		Bn. Training & preparing to move up into Front Line	
"	6/4/16			

Army Form C. 2118.

WAR DIARY
or
INTELLIGENCE SUMMARY.
(Erase heading not required.)

Instructions regarding War Diaries and Intelligence Summaries are contained in F. S. Regs., Part II. and the Staff Manual respectively. Title pages will be prepared in manuscript.

Place	Date	Hour	Summary of Events and Information	Remarks and references to Appendices
FRANCE ACHEUX	12/4/16	—	Spent day preparing to relieve 1st Border Regt. in Front Line Trenches. Weather very bad. Left ACHEUX at 7.40pm marched (as Battalion) to AUCHONVILLERS — about 1000 x behind Firing Line. Trenches very muddy & slippery — relief completed by 0230 on 13/4/16. Front line taken over about 1200 x long in 4 Coyfront X, Y, & Z (in that order from left flank) in Firing Line. Casualties — Nil. Support Coy in Firing Line. Casualties — Nil.	Effective Strength Offs. O.R. 25 908 "Strength
AUCHONVILLERS (Firing Line)	13/4/16	—	Raining all day — trenches almost impassable in consequence. Whole Bn engaged clearing, draining & improving trenches — especially Front Line & Communication trenches. Emergency guide. Casualties Nil.	25 965
AUCHONVILLERS	14/4/16	—	Weather clearing — men working very well, for the most part, trenches very much improved. Revetting attempted now in 2nd line trenches. Casualties Nil.	" 965
— do —	15/4/16	—	Working hard on 2nd Line — great deal of work to be done as the line was practically without traverses. Z Coy (Capt RILEY) ↕ especially looking well. Casualties Nil. Last evening 2nd Line troops — also commenced the digging of a new Fire Trench about 40x in front of old Fire Trench SANDY ROW 1st Q.45. Very good work by Z Coy (Capt. Riley). Casualties Nil.	25 965 26 955
— do —	16/4/16	—	— Support from SANDY ROW 1st Q.45 — Very good work by Z Coy (Capt. Riley) — Casualties — Nil. Consolidation on new Firing Line trench. Traversed rift opened up & right through & lightly held — but not fire swept.	—
— do —	17/4/16	—	Shift made up & for traverse completed. Casualties No 7530 Pte J. CAMPBELL "Killed" gunshot wound — chest (Bn of enemy party in front of new Trench). ⊕ 7.30 Pte J. CAMPBELL "Killed" gunshot	26 954

⊕ 2/Lt. F. MILLER 3rd R.D.F. joined up with this Bn. & posted to X Coy (formerly attached R.F.C.).

2/Lt F. MILLER

Army Form C. 2118.

WAR DIARY
or
INTELLIGENCE SUMMARY.
(Erase heading not required.)

Instructions regarding War Diaries and Intelligence Summaries are contained in F. S. Regs., Part II. and the Staff Manual respectively. Title pages will be prepared in manuscript.

Place	Date	Hour	Summary of Events and Information	Remarks and references to Appendices
AUCHONVILLERS (Firing Line)	18/4/16		Very bad weather - trenches in bad state. Work on new firing line continued - Lad progress naturally very slow. Z Coy relieved by Coy of Worcester (4th) sent to Reserve. W Coy relieved a Coy of 1st Lancashire Fusiliers on our left. Plans to hold this new front from BG/34 to left F & 10 Coy on right. Casualties - Nil.	String Q.L. 26 - 9.54
"	19/4/16		Weather - had a wet fragrant chiefly to snowgrain. Casualties - No 16308 Pte COLE (shrapnel - hit just as he was leaving Reg'l Dressing Station).	26 - 9.46
"	20/4/16		No improvement in weather - if anything the reverse. Very difficult to make any headway with trench work. Trenches very wet and bad for traffic. Casualties - Nil.	26 - 9.44
"	21/4/16		Weather continues bad - work practically abandoned. Impossible to work owing to slate of ground. Lt A.W. FREW attached to Bn. Tim Capt L.D. SHAW R.A.M.C. transferred to 89th Field Ambulance. Received orders for relief by Bn. of Royal Fusiliers. Casualties - Nil.	26 - 9.44
"	22/4/16		Weather showed signs of clearing. Relieved by 9th Royal Fusiliers - Relief completed by midnight. Casualties - No 9532 Pte COX (Dysentery). Drummer Sgt. at last arrived & started to Bn for duty.	25 - 9.30
MAILLY MAILLET	23/4/16		Arrived in Reserve Billets very early in morning. Day off for all Ranks except 2 Coy's (infantry) 1 Co dig at Suffcroft). Y Co digging New 1st Avenue Communication Trench - at night. Casualties - Sergt. A Chevallier - Lt Sergt I Barber - Lt Sergt I Chevallier - No 5729 Pte SWIN (Heart Failure).	27 - 9.00

WAR DIARY
or
INTELLIGENCE SUMMARY.

Army Form C. 2118.

Instructions regarding War Diaries and Intelligence Summaries are contained in F. S. Regs., Part II. and the Staff Manual respectively. Title pages will be prepared in manuscript.

(Erase heading not required.)

Place	Date	Hour	Summary of Events and Information	Remarks and references to Appendices
MAILLET MAILLET	24/4/16		Bn. in Reserve Billets and digging trench. Work in hand improving & completing 5th Avenue, Parts of 2nd Avenue, St Helen's Rd (also converting these into Fire Trench). Casualties - Nil	27 – 897
–do–	25/4/16		Still in Reserve – working very hard all night & parts of day. Casualties Nil	27 – 887
–do–	26/4/16		–do– day 1 in night. Lt. R.G.A. Guns Cunningham (3/859) gazed	28 – 886
–do–			The Bn. Casualties Nil	
–do–	27/4/16		Still in Reserve. Reserve advance orders for Bn. F.Gs in Corps Reserve as soon as work in Trench (on above) is completed. Men looking very well. Casualties Nil	26 – 886
–do–	28/4/16		Work completed. Bn. Employed as escort by G.O.C. Division (Gen. de Lisle). Preparing to move into Corps Reserve at LOUVENCOURT. Left at 2000. Reached LOUVENCOURT at 2220. No one fell out on line of march. Casualties Nil	28 – 879
LOUVENCOURT	29/4/16		Bn. in Corps Reserve. Very heavy working parties to be found every second day (450 men). Remainder of Bn. (3 whole Cos on alternate days) employed in training – mainly in specialist work. Bombing. Lewis Mg work. Signalling. Scouting. Sniping. Bayonet fighting. Wiring & musketry. Casualties Nil. Capt. R.L.B.W.	29 – 879
	30/4/16		M.O.? reported B. Capt. Armstrong to left company (in true Lecht Mason) (on leave) Lt Corps Reserve. Casualties – Nil	29 – 877
	1/5/16		–do–	29 – 879

O U T P O S T S.

**HEADQUARTERS,
86th
INFANTRY BRIGADE.**
No. D 2 670
Date...................

1. The following is the line to be held by outposts in the vicinity of Beauval.

One Company, 1.R.Dublin Fusiliers from Pt.144 (inclusive) ¼ mile due North of V in BEAUVAL to Pt.91 (exclusive) ½ mile N.E. of BEAUVAL.

One Company, 2nd Royal Fusiliers, from Pt.91 (inclusive) to Pt.95 (exclusive) one mile E. of BEAUVAL.

One Company, R.Munster Fusiliers, Point 95 (inclusive) to Pt.101 (inclusive) ¾ mile N.W. of BEAUQUESNE.

2. Officers Commanding Units concerned will send an Officer as soon as possible to their area and arrange disposition of their companies.

3. There will be no O.C., Outposts. Officers Commanding Outpost Companies will report direct/to their Commanding Officers.

4. This line will not actually be held *unless ordered*.

1/4/16.

C.M.Williams
Capt.,
~~Staff Captain~~, 86th Bde.
Brigade Major,

"A" Form.
Army Form C. 2121.

MESSAGES AND SIGNALS.

No. of Message _____

Prefix _____ Code _____ m.
Office of Origin and Service Instructions

SECRET.

Words | Charge
Sent
At _____ m.
To _____
By _____

This message is on a/c of:
_____ Service.
(Signature of "Franking Officer.")

Recd. at _____ m.
Date _____
From _____
By _____

TO { ALL BATTALIONS

Sender's Number. | Day of Month. | In reply to Number | AAA
B.M.176. | 7th | |

THE BRIGADIER HAS DECIDED THAT HE WILL PROBABLY HOLD THE LINE WITH FOUR BATTALIONS EACH FINDING THEIR OWN SUPPORTS RESERVES ETC. ETC. LOTS WERE DRAWN FOR POSITIONS IN THE LINE AND THE ORDER AS UNDER DECIDED ON FROM RIGHT TO LEFT R. MUNSTER FUSILIERS ROYAL FUSILIERS R. DUBLIN FUSILIERS LANCASHIRE FUSILIERS OFFICERS SHOULD VISIT PROBABLE FRONTAGE TO BE OCCUPIED BY THEIR OWN BATTALIONS AAA AFTER LAST NIGHT'S ACTION IT APPEARS ADVISABLE NOT TO WORRY THE LINE AT PRESENT HELD BY S.W.B'S WITH SIGHTSEERS. AAA ADDRESSED ALL BATTALIONS

From
Place 86th BRIGADE.
Time 0935

The above may be forwarded as now corrected.   (Z)
Censor.   Signature of Addresser or person authorised to telegraph in his name.
* This line should be erased if not required.

"A" Form.
MESSAGES AND SIGNALS

Army Form C. 2121.

Prefix	Code	m.	Words	Charge	This message is on a/c of:	Recd. at	m.
Office of Origin and Service Instructions.			Sent			Date	
			At	m.	Service.	From	
			To			By	
			By		(Signature of "Franking Officer.")		

TO.

Sender's Number.	Day of Month	In reply to Number	AAA

taking over from Lancs Fusiliers will be notified later. Batt'n H.Q'rs will remain in its present position. Officers Commanding W. X. Y Companies will please inspect the new line to be taken over by them and report what dug-out accommodation there is available.

RB/CG

O.C. Z & W Coys. Please initial last named & return.

H. Nelson Weld
Commd'g 1. Royal Dublin Fusiliers.

2235.
17/4/16

From: ...
Place: X
Time: 10.45 A.M.

"A" Form.   Army Form C. 2121.
                    MESSAGES AND SIGNALS   No. of Message_____

Prefix ___ Code ___ m.	Words	Charge	This message is on a/c of:	Recd. at _____ m.
Office of Origin and Service Instructions.				Date_____
	Sent		_____Service.	From_____
	At _____ m.			
	To _____			
___	By _____		(Signature of "Franking Officer.")	By _____

| TO | all Companies. | | |
| | | | |

| Sender's Number. | Day of Month | In reply to Number | A A A |

Owing to 88th Brigade taking over part of the line held by the 86th. the line held at present by Companies will be altered. The new line to be held by the Battalion is from the new BEAUMONT ROAD Q.4.4. (at Trench map) to E St. Q.10.5. 4 Companies will take up the line as follows. W Company on relief by 4th Worcesters will take over from Lancs Fus from NEW BEAUMONT ROAD to Q.10.16. X Company from Q.10.16 to Q.10.9. Y Company from Q.10.9 to Q.10.5. Z Company will be in Batt'n Reserve: at a place to be notified later. The O.C's. W & Z Coys will hand over all their trench stores taken over by them to the Worcester Regt. Re O.C Y Coy will hand over such proportion of trench stores as are now in the line that portion of their line to be taken over by the Worcesters, & will take over from O.C X Coy such proportion of the latters stores belonging to that portion of the line to be taken over by Y Company. Details regarding time of

From		
Place		
Time		
The above may be forwarded as now corrected.   (Z)
_____
              Censor.   Signature of Addresser or person authorised to telegraph in his name.
                   * This line should be erased if not required.
—M&C. & Co. Ltd., London.— W 11400/2045. 100,000. 2/15. Forms C 2121/10.

To 1/R.D.F.

Under instructions from G.O.C. Div'n you are to complete tonight a fire trench from Q.10.10 to Q.10.4 as shown in red on the enclosed map. The trench must be wired in front & fit for occupation & held tomorrow. All other work must give way to this and a very great point made to see it completed.

Acknowledge.

1320
17/4/16

Ian Grant Capt
Bde Major 86th Bde.

Wire on receipt of this assistance that can be rendered by brigade reference materiel etc or in any other respects with regard to this work.

Ian Grant Capt.
Bde Major 86th Bde.

"C" Form (Duplicate).
MESSAGES AND SIGNALS.

SM KA 60

Office Stamp: AXU 18-4-16

Handed in at AX

TO AXU

BM343 18th
Ref Par 1 BDE Orders No 46
of 17th inst for Q10/5
Mead Junction Q10/7 and
Q10/6 AAA Ref 1/10000 map
BEAUMONT Southern Boundary
of SECTOR is LIMERICK
JUNCTION FIRST AVENUE
TIPPERARY AVENUE to Railway
(All inclusive to LEFT SECTOR)
Then along 140 Contour to
the road joining VITERMONT
and MAILLY

FROM / PLACE & TIME: 86th Bde 0950

"A" Form. Army Form C. 2121.

MESSAGES AND SIGNALS.

Prefix SM Code 4CP m.	Words 54	Charge	This message is on a/c of	Recd. at 4.30 p m.
Office of Origin and Service Instructions.	Sent At ___ m. To ✓ By ___		___ Service. ✓ (Signature of "Franking Officer.")	AXU Date 21-4-16 From AX By Pte Jones S.A
AXR				

TO AXU

Sender's Number.	Day of Month	In reply to Number	AAA
RF 36	21st/4		

Reference tomorrow relief AAA
M Company for left half of
line leaves here at 1900
and Company for right Half
at 1930 AAA no guides will
be required AAA please
let me have your
log book AAA parties for
mining and dugouts will
report to yours at 10.30

From
Place AXR
Time

The above may be forwarded as now corrected. (Z)

Censor. Signature of Addressee or person authorised to telegraph in his name.

* This line should be erased if not required.

"A" Form.   Army Form C. 2121.
MESSAGES AND SIGNALS   No. of Message _____

Prefix SA Code GLP m.	Words 75	Charge	This message is on a/c of	Recd. at 8.16 p.m.
Office of Origin and Service Instructions. AX	Sent At ___ m. To ___ By ___		_____ Service. Telephone (Signature of "Franking Officer.")	Date 26.4.16 From AX By Pte Green

TO	AXU		
Sender's Number. S6616	Day of Month 21st	In reply to Number 1815	A A A

The following reliefs are to
take place 0930 tomorrow.
Battle Police & Baths sanitary squads
Bath House duties Town Major
orderlys Town Police AAA all guards
AAA Fire picquet of 4 NCO +
6 men AAA Guards mount with
sidearms and sticks AAA Your
water guard will be relieved at
9.30 am and the mining party
at 7 pm all other working parties
on relief of Batts.

✱ Town

From	AX
Place	
Time	1945

O/C 1.R. Dublin Ins? 20/4/16

With reference to my message last night about "log-book" — I am not going into your Head Qrs at all, but straight into others at point where 2nd AVENUE leaves the OLD BEAUMONT Road — but as your log book refers to the line I am taking over, the G O C wishes me to have it, & not the C O who will occupy your Hd. Qrs. My Sergt Major is taking this note to you, to see about taking over Hd. Qr stuff (ammunition &c), so could you give him the book to bring to me, or arrange to have it sent to my Hd Qrs this evening? Unless there is anything special you wish to discuss, I do not propose to come to your Hd. Qrs tonight as I shall have plenty to do at my own

S Johnson Lt Col
Cdg 2 R F

O/C 9 R∴ F

Ref your 0950 of 22nd

I propose to have 2 Coys in firing line finding own supports + 2 Coys at Auchonvillers — my Coys are fairly strong.

H Johnson Lt Col
[dg 2 R F]

C O P Y.

To:-
   Staff Captain,
      86th Brigade.

LIST OF DUTIES FOUND BY BATTALION.

Battle Police (3 Posts)	3 Sergts. &	18 men
Town Sanitary Squads	1 N.C.O. &	7 men
Bath-house Duties	1 N.C.O. &	2 men
Town Major's Orderlies		2 men
Town Police		3 men
Duty of 87th Field Ambulance in SALLE de REUNION	1 N.C.O. &	3 men
Baker for town		1 man
TOTALS	6 N.C.Os. &	36 men

G U A R D S.

No. 1 Control Post	1 N.C.O. - 1 Bugler &	3 men	W
" II " "	1 N.C.O. &	3 men	X
Aeroplane Observation Post	1 N.C.O. 1 Bugler &	3 men	Y
Brigade H.Q. Guard.	1 N.C.O. &	3 men	Z
TOTAL.	4 N.C.Os. 2 Buglers &	12 men	

F A T I G U E S.

Washing Gum Boots at Bde. Dump.		4 men (9 a.m. & 2 p.m.)
C.R.E. Dump Fatigue	1 N.C.O. &	12 men (9 a.m.)
Heavy Battery	1 N.C.O. &	14 men (9 a.m.)
TOTAL	2 N.C.Os &	30 men

Attached to West Riding R.E.   10 men (I understand these are to remain)

PICQUET.

Fire Picquet   1 Officer, 4 N.C.Os. and 50 men.

****

These reliefs are to report to Royal Fusiliers Headquarters by 0930 tomorrow.

21/4/16.   Sd./ G.C. Pearson, Lieut: & Adjt:,
                                2nd Royal Fusiliers.

Please comply.

HEADQUARTERS,
86th
INFANTRY BRIGADE.

Memo
BM 35

1/Royal Dublin Fus.

1. I am instructed by the Brigadier to request that you will put on all available men to dig a communication trench, as shown in Red on the attached sketch.

2. The trench should be reconnoitred and marked out by one of your officers, tracing tape being procured for the purpose.

3. 1st Avenue should start approx. 2 telegraph poles N of the Western end of TIPPERARY AVENUE, and an entirely new route cut to where the existing 1st Avenue joins the BROADWAY.

4. Work can only be carried out at night

5. Dimensions as under

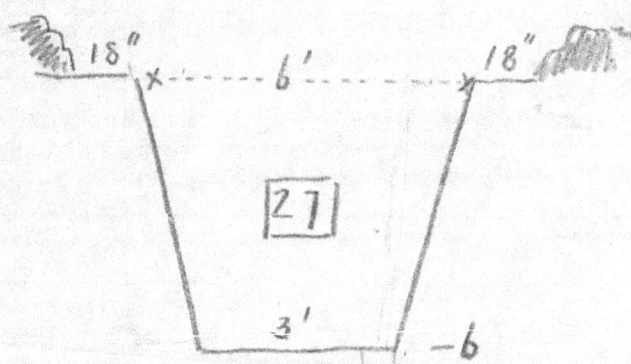

BM. 35

5 (cont'd) There is approx 900ˣ to be cut
i.e. 27 × 900 × 3 c. feet
Each man should excavate 40 c. feet per day
The Brigadier assumes that you can work
a minimum of 400 men a night.

At this rate the work should, tho
under normal weather conditions, be
completed in the 5 nights prior to the
relief of this Bde.

$$\left[e.g.\ \frac{27 \times 900 \times 3}{400 \times 40} = 4.55 \text{ nights work} \right]$$

6. The trench should be zig-zagged and
steps cut leading out at 75ˣ
interval on alternate sides, and
a drain cut along
one side if time permits

7. In addition please detail daily,
day work
1 N.C.O and 6   Work W end Broadway
to Pompadour

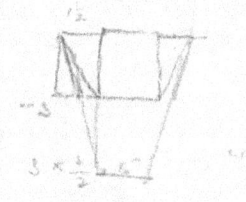

7(cont) 1 officer and 20 men to work on 2nd Avenue between AUCHONVILLERS and Hdqrs 2/Royal Fus

8. All other available men to be employed working in 5th Avenue :- which is to be improved to the same dimensions as shown in para 5

Ian Grant. Capt
Bde Major 86/Bde

22 4/16.

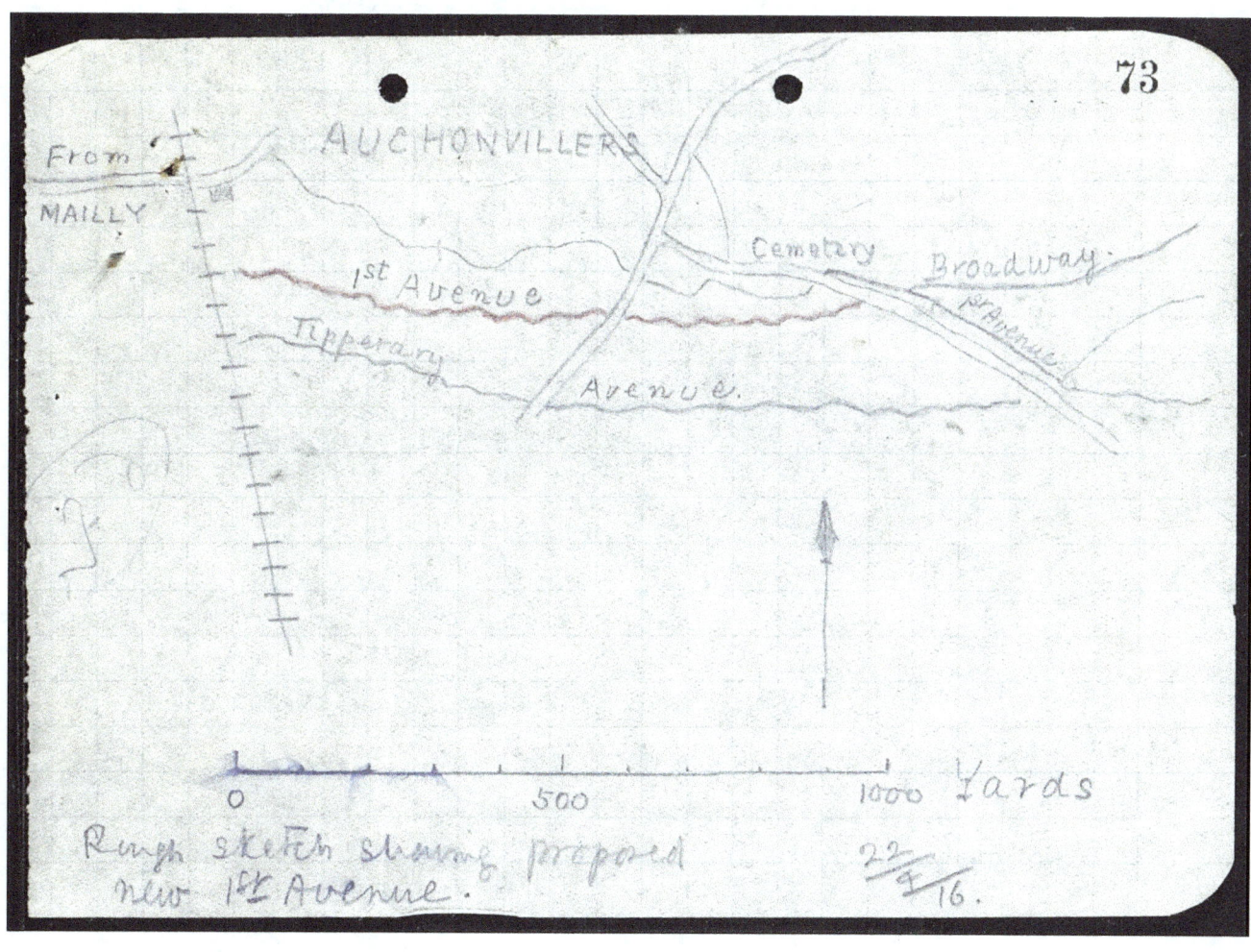

VERY URGENT.

> HEADQUARTERS,
> 86th
> INFANTRY BRIGADE.
> No. D.1037
> Date. 24/4/16

O.C.,
  1.R.Dublin Fus.

1. In addition to the completion of the 5th Avenue, mentioned in my D.1035 of date, the G.O.C. Division considers that the work mentioned below should be completed before relief. Work will, therefore, be re-allotted as follows:-

2. FRONT LINE.

By Garrison. (1). Improving front line trenches, deepening the footway to at least 3' below the fire step and widening it to 2' at the bottom.

(2). Digging out saps to the front and continuing these beyond the wire - in some cases these saps have been filled in, noticeably so in the Northern Sector. They must be dug out forthwith.

(3). Deepening and making into a fire trench the cut from Q.4.7 to Q.4.9.

(4). Draining and deepening 2nd Avenue East of 2nd Royal Fusiliers Headquarters and Pilk Street.

3. 1.R.Dublin Fus*rs.
  5th Avenue to be drained; side exits cut and deepened.
  CARDIFF St & St HELEN'S Junction. OLD BEAUMONT
  St.Helens Street to be prepared as a fire trench.

  1.Lancashire Fus.
  2nd Avenue West of 2nd Royal Fusiliers to be drained and deepened, and side steps cut.

  Cardiff Street to be prepared as a fire trench and the North end of the former to be connected with Q.4.3; in this connection the old Beaumont Road will not be cut through but tunnelled under and propped.

4. This work cannot be completed unless men are worked to full extent and the work well organized; tasks should be calculated at 40 cubic feet per diem per man.

Water must be drained off by cuts into lower ground or sumps. Much of the work in rear of the front line must be carried out by night. Officers in charge of working parties must be given the work to be done by day, otherwise time is lost and labour wasted.

24/4/1916.

Captain,
Brigade Major, 86th Infy.Bde.

O.C., 1 R Dub Fus.

During the period the Brigade is in Corps Reserve, the front line training will be carried out as far as possible as follows, it being realised that 850 men are employed daily on fatigue from the Brigade.

1. Daily before breakfasts all ranks, including specialists, will carry out physical exercises and running drill for half an hour followed by half an hour musketry and muscle exercises. Any loose order dress.

2. Daily at least half an hour close order drill.

3. Battalions will carry out a route march every other day - without packs - commencing at 8 miles and increasing to 12: roads will be allotted. First line transport will always march with battalions. One Brigade Route March will be arranged.

4. Each battalion will detail a party of 2 officers and 40 other ranks to carry out a raid into hostile trenches. Orders for the raid will be written out precisely, and the raid practised both by day and night on several occasions.

5. In addition to being first a soldier, every man in the battalion must be trained as a specialist. The following specialists will receive instruction:-
   Men for wiring and wire cutting.
   Signallers and runners.
   Men for revetment work.
   Snipers and observers.
   Patrols.
   Bombers.

   Every man in the battalion should be a bomber, and in addition a special bombing company will be formed and trained under the Brigade Bombing Officer.

6. Where trenches are available, an attack from them must be practised, i.e. leaving the trenches, carrying ladders and bridges, crossing trenches, wire cutting.

7. The 29th inst. will be employed checking equipment, clothing, gas helmets, iron rations, etc., also cleaning up at the discretion of Battalion Commanders.

   It is hoped to carry out the following inter-battalion competitions:-
   1. Wiring competition.
   2. Patrolling competition.
   3. Grenadier competition.
   4. Sniping competition.
   5. Revetting competition.

28/4/16.

Captain,
Brigade Major, 86th Brigade.

1st. Royal Dublin Fusiliers

[*Crown copyright reserved*

NOTES FOR THE ASSISTANCE OF TROOPS IN DEALING WITH SPIES.

The following notes are issued for assistance of troops dealing with espionage:—

1. At Rheims a case occurred where civilians were caught signalling to German troops on the high ground round the town by means of lights, coloured and otherwise, placed at night in windows.

2. Signals have also been sent by intermittent smoke from chimneys.

3. Near Rheims an underground telephone line was found connecting with the enemy's lines, which was used by a German spy.

4. Several women spies have been caught collecting information regarding names and numbers of regiments, numbers of officers, &c.

5. Spies have been caught at railhead observing entrainment and detrainment of troops.

6. The keeping of unregistered carrier pigeons is illegal, and they are a favourite method of communication by spies. On arrival in a village an order should be given to the Maire that all cages are to be opened and cellars searched for pigeons. Civilians on the road should also be searched for pigeons, as these latter are sometimes carried in the pocket.

7. An easy means by which spies can approach our lines is in company with refugees. These latter should therefore be questioned by the police, and should not be allowed to enter the area occupied by the troops.

8. Labourers working in the fields between the armies have been detected giving information.

9. People in civilian clothes following our troops when retiring have acted as advanced scouts to German cavalry. A similar procedure may be expected when we are advancing.

10. It is known that German officers and men in plain clothes, or in French or English uniform, have remained in localities evacuated by their armies. French and British stragglers should therefore be handed over to the police.

[P.T.O.

ORDERS AS TO PROCEDURE TO BE ADOPTED ON ENTERING A FRENCH TOWN OR VILLAGE.

1. Order the Maire or the official representing him to post the proclamation restricting the movement of inhabitants, and inform him that he is responsible that its tenour is known and that the risks run by non-compliance are understood.

2. Order the Maire to make a house-to-house search for concealed pigeons, and to open pigeon cages.

3. Institute enquiries amongst the inhabitants as to any suspicious characters, and find out if there are any recent arrivals.

4. Ask if any inhabitants have been seen talking to Germans during the latter's occupation—this especially applies to women.

5. Ascertain which hotels and cafés remained open and direct particular attention to these establishments.

6. Ascertain if there are any telephones working in the direction of the enemy.
Issue orders that all private telephone lines are disconnected.

7. Watch for any suspicious lights or any intermittent smoke.

8. Any person on whom the least suspicion rests should be handed over to the nearest French police, or failing them, to the nearest French troops.
It should be borne in mind that even if no conviction can be secured, a spy's information is rendered worthless if delayed. The moral effect of frequent arrests is the best safeguard against spies.

9. Spies caught red-handed should, after trial, be shot, a record of the evidence being kept.

C. F. N. MACREADY, *Lieut.-General,*
Adjutant-General British Army in the Field.

Operation Orders. No 1.
by
Lieut. Col. H. Nelson, D.S.O.
Commanding 1 Rl. Dub. Fus.
Thursday 28th April 1916.

1. The Battalion will move to Louvencourt to night. Coys. will rendezvous at the cross roads P.12 C.9 on Forceville Road at 19.55. The order of march will be :- Pioneers, Signallers, W X Y Z Coys, Bombers, Machine Gunners. The Battalion will proceed to Louvencourt as soon as the leading Battalion of the 87th Brigade has passed the cross roads referred to above.

2. All Class B men, and Light Duty men will parade at Bn. Hd. Qrs. at 1730, by Coys. under Lieut. D.R. Warner. This officer will be responsible for getting the party to Louvencourt.

3. Coy. Mess Boxes will be at Bn. H.Q. at 1915.

4. Transport will be despatched by day, two waggons at a time, under the orders of the Quartermaster.

5. O/C. Coys are requested to have all Tools returned to Bn. H. Qrs. at once.

6. Bn. Reserve S.A.A., all Helmets, Tools & Cookers will be handed over to the relieving Battalion.

7. Lt. G.L. Jacobs will remain behind and inspect all billets occupied by the Battalion. He will then report to the Staff Captain, 86th Bde. and, if necessary, accompany him round the billets.

8. O/C. Coys. will send an officer to Bn. H. Qrs. to report when their respective companies are settled in billets at Louvencourt.

9. 2/Lt. W.V. Spankie will march in rear of the Bn.

Much fighting abt E ends of J 12 and J 13 during night.

and will collect and bring
into Lawrencourt, as a formed
body, all stragglers and men
who drop out on the line
of march to-night.

F.A. Wilson Lieut.
28.4.16. a/adjt. 1/R.D.F.

"A" Branch

2nd Low.Fd.

of 4/1st

4th C of G

both trenches

2/nd Low.

the beach

Bde. Diary
155th Inf.

ront, esp.

10.15pm.

4/21st.

5 cas. from

p. from gun

5/21st.

4/25th.

O.C. 1st R.Dublin Fus.

1. In event of serious attack, the Brigade must be prepared to move forward and occupy the brown or Corps line (see attached sketch). Units will arrange that the routes, lines of approach, etc. to their line be reconnoitred by Company officers, transport officers, etc.

Battalions will reconnoitre the sections marked on the attached sketch as under:-

    Section A:... 1.Lancashire Fusrs.
    "   B:... 1.R.Dublin Fusrs.
    "   C:... 16th Middlesex & 2nd Royal Fusrs.

29/4/16.

Capt.,
Brigade Major, 86th Bde.

29th Division.

In reply to your G.O.93 of today, the attached is the proposed scheme of work for the Brigade between the 3rd and 5th May.

Daily working parties, now called for, amount to 850 rank and file, which precludes systematic training beyond that of specialists.

The 2nd Royal Fusiliers and 1st R.Dublin Fusiliers will be at LOUVENCOURT; the 1st Lancashire Fusiliers and 16th Mⁱddlesex Regt. at ACHEUX.

                        (Signed) W.L.Williams, Brigadier Genrl.,
28th April, 1916.   Commanding 86th Infantry Brigade.

The following are the specialist classes in hand under Brigade arrangements apart from those under battalion arrangements.

1. Four officers 160 other ranks provisional Brigade Grenadier Company, under Brigade Grenadier Officer.

2. Four officers and 32 corporals and sergeants training as instructors.

3. Course on Gas, 1st-5th May. Eight N.C.O's under Divisional Gas Adviser.

                        (Signed) A.V.JOHNSON, Lt-Col.,
29/4/1916.   Commanding 86th Infy.Bde.

29th Division.
86th Infantry Brigade.
6

MAY & JUNE 1916

1st BATTALION

ROYAL DUBLIN FUSILIERS

M A Y & J U N E 1 9 1 6

MAY & JUNE 1916 — 8th Roy Dublin Fusiliers

WAR DIARY or INTELLIGENCE SUMMARY

Army Form C. 2118.

Place	Date	Hour	Summary of Events and Information	Remarks and references to Appendices
LOUVENCOURT	2/5/16		Bn. still in Corps Reserve. Time employed in working parties of various Bn. Commanders	* 4 Lt T.R. OXLEY transferred (Postal) to 8th T.M. Battery with effect from 1/5/16. 29 – 8.7.4
-do-	3/4/16		-do-	* above. 28 – 8.7.4
-do-	4/4/16		-do-	28 – 8.7.7
-do-	5/5/16		-do- Capt. H. BRUCE (M.O.7) & Corps H.Q. 7th Wilts on joined Bn.	29 – 9.4.9
			2nd Lieut. C.E. HAWES appointed to 9th Divisional School (Capt. BRUCE takes over Y Coy)	Strength including M.O. & 1st Chaplain 30 – 9.4.9
			Bn. still in Corps Reserve. Practically whole Bn. on working parties. Casualties Nil.	31 – 9.4.8
-do-	6/5/16		-do- 2/Lt H. GREEN taken on strength 4th Bn (July 3)	
-do-	7/5/16		-do- No work. Orders to take over portion of Firing Line held by 1/Essex.	
-do-	8/5/16		Relief carried out by Coys. X (on left) in Front Line; W Y Z in support (at AUCHONVILLERS) Relief complete by 2130. Capt. LAW taken over W Coy.	
FIRING LINE near AUCHONVILLERS	9/5/16		Weather changed – fairly heavy rain fell – trenches quite bad – trouble to do several work in consequence. Bn. holds Line from O.6.7 (on Right) to R.M.2 (left), being Right of Left Sub-Section.	31 – 9.4.8
-do-	10/5/16		Weather improving – Trenches Likewise. Bn. working cleaning up, improving things in & Support Line & Communication Trenches - especially 2nd Avenue. Enemy very quiet. Casualties Nil.	31 – 9.4.5
-do-	11/5/16		Trenches almost dry - work progressing well. Made a start to ESSEX ST. (new lead). Enemy quiet - very little sniping or shelling. Casualties Nil. 4th Lt J.C. DEVOY 1/R.D.F. joined B. 4.	32 – 9.4.5

Army Form C. 2118.

WAR DIARY
or
INTELLIGENCE SUMMARY.
(Erase heading not required.)

Instructions regarding War Diaries and Intelligence Summaries are contained in F. S. Regs., Part II. and the Staff Manual respectively. Title pages will be prepared in manuscript.

Place	Date	Hour	Summary of Events and Information	Remarks and references to Appendices
FIRING LINE AUCHONVILLERS	11/3/16		Z Coy moved to R.E.S Trench. Four from AUCHON—	
	12/3/16		Trenches dry. Work progressing apace. Special attention to be given to Bridge Traverses. Lieut. E. de LISLE, Casualties No. 52 – 942	52 – 942
			Weather had open – Trenches very muddy – work stopped. W Coy relieved X Coy. Z Coy relieved Y Coy. X Coy became garrison of AUCHON. 2/9 Y Coy went to POMPADOUR. 85TH TRENCH to CARDIFF ST. Relief complete by 20.00. LT. JACOBS G.L. (to hospital) struck off strength of J. Br. Capt. E.R.L. MAINSELL 9/R.O.F. & Capt. P. de B. DALY M/R.O.F. taken on strength & posted to Z & X Coy resply Casualties —	53 – 938
-do-	14/3/16		Z Coy carrying fatigues and Casualties Nil.	
-do-	15/3/16		Fine but weather – work stopped in consequence.	Casualties Nil. 53 – 938
-do-	16/3/16		Weather improving & work recommenced. Attention being paid chiefly to finishing Bridge Traverses in the new Communication Trenches & cleaning & improving 2ND AVENUE. Draft of 50 men Casualties Nil.	33 – 777
-do-	16/3/16		Trenches drying up well & work progressing. Working chiefly on Sandbag Traverses down the Comm'n Trenches near Junct. w/n No.1 & No.2 AVENUES, ESSEX ST, X ST, PALL ST, 85TH TRENCH Y & 2ND AVENUE continued. 2/LT. FISHER left for LONDON under orders to report at War Office — Casualties Nil	52 – 777
-do-	17/3/16		Fine weather – Trenches dry & a considerable amount of work done. LT. R. ELDWICK Y/R.D.F. & LT. W.E. CHADWICK joined the Bn. & posted to Z & X respectively. Casualties other rank 1 Bn. of Somt. 34 —	715
			Two Welsh whom killed on 16 inst.	
			Bn. relieved by 1st Royal Fusiliers; relief completed by 19.00. Casualties NIL Bn. billets in MAILLY (no no 34) – 2nd Bn. Hants —	77.5

Army Form C. 2118.

WAR DIARY
or
INTELLIGENCE SUMMARY.
(Erase heading not required.)

Instructions regarding War Diaries and Intelligence Summaries are contained in F.S. Regs., Part II. and the Staff Manual respectively. Title pages will be prepared in manuscript.

Place	Date	Hour	Summary of Events and Information	Remarks and references to Appendices
MAILLY MAILLET	19/5/16		As Divisional Reserve stood to find permanent working parties totalling over 500 men. Remainder of Bn. working on BROADWAY, ESSEX ST, 2ND AVENUE & PILK ST. Casualties Nil.	34 – 993
-do-	20/5/16		Work continued – as above. Capt F.R. COLLINS & LT. J.N. BARRY joined Bn. & posted to Z & X Coys respectively. Casualties - Nil.	36 - 993
-do-	21/5/16		Day of Rest – except for Working Party. Casualties – Nil	36 – 994
-do-	22/5/16 to		Whole Bn. working – on trenches & works mentioned above. Strength 22/5/16	36 – 989
	28/5/16		Capt. M. de B. DALY to Hospital on 24/5/16 (Sickness). Casualties Nil. Bn. moved down to Corps Res. LOUVENCOURT – Relieved by Newfoundland Regt.	28/5/16 35 – 980
LOUVENCOURT	29/5/16		Bn. all out working finding Corps working parties of over 700 men. Casualties Nil.	35 – 986
-do-	30/5/16		-do-	35 – 983
-do-	31/5/16		Bn. relieved of most working parties. Commenced Training. Draft of 99 O.R. arrived – Casualties Nil	35 – 1062
-do-	1/6/16		Training operations continued.	-do- 35 – 1059
-do-	2/6/16		-do-	-do- 35 - 1059
-do-	3/6/16		-do-	-do- 35 – 1059
-do-	4/6/16		Day of Rest. Brigade Exercise	-do- 35 – 1061
-do-	5/6/16		Brigade Exercise & Demonstration	-do- 35 – 1060
-do-	6/6/16		Brigade Exercise – Orders to relieve 1st Essex Regt. in Front Line – tomorrow.	-do- 35 – 1059

Brigade Exercise

1577 Wt.W10791/1773 500,000 1/15 D.D. & L. A.D.S.S./Forms/C. 2118.

WAR DIARY
or
INTELLIGENCE SUMMARY.
(Erase heading not required.)

Army Form C. 2118.

Instructions regarding War Diaries and Intelligence Summaries are contained in F. S. Regs., Part II. and the Staff Manual respectively. Title pages will be prepared in manuscript.

Place	Date	Hour	Summary of Events and Information	Remarks and references to Appendices
LOUVENCOURT	7/8/16		Morning spent preparing to move up to Front Line : afternoon relieved 11th Essex Rgt. in Firing Line — Relief completed by 1800. Following Officers joined Bn. 4/8/16 G.V. WICKHAM (M.G.), C.M. McFEELEY (W), McTIGHE (X) & I.D. MACKENZIE (Y)	
FIRING LINE	8/8/16			Casualties - NIL 39 - 1059
HEBUTERNE VILLERS			Greater part of Front Line was held during last Tour. Rain commenced — work cleaning & draining trenches & making latrines. Gun emplacements in front of parapet. Draft of 25 other Ranks arrived.	Casualties - Nil 39 - 1082
-do-	9/8/16		Weather still very bad & work held up in consequence.	-do- 39 - 1022
-do-	10/8/16		Weather improving — work continued. Some enemy trench mortars Reconnoitring Patrol (Lt. C.B. DAVIES, No. —— Sgt. —— No. —— Pte HAYDEN v Pte DUNNE) went out into Norman's Land and only one (No. —— Pte DUNNE returned) the rest severely wounded.	38 - 1076
-do-	11/8/16		Weather had again — Day of rest. Draft of 5 other ranks arrived. The band of —— public Casualties No.	38 - 1050
-do-	12/8/16		The improvement in weather. Y Coy relieved W & latter went into Reserve, Z Coy relieved X & latter to Support. Relief completed by 1700. Lt. J.A. CLARKE joined Bn. & posted to Z Coy.	Casualties - Nil 39 - 1073
-do-	13/8/16		Weather as bad as ever. Capt. C.E. HAYNES taken an alarmingly severe (Y Coy) & shown as on Command while employed as Instructor at Divisional School ACHEUX	Casualties No 40 - 1074
-do-	14/8/16		No change — Capt. W.P. OULTON rejoined Bn. & posted to X Coy.	-do- 41 - 1074
-do-	15/8/16		Relieved by 2nd Royal Fusiliers. Relief completed by 1600. Bn. moved in Reserve in MAILLY WOOD (Mily). Major SEYMOUR joined Bn. & assumed Comd of 2nd in Command. Capt. J.S. TRIGONG took over Command of Z Coy.	42 - 1072

Army Form C. 2118.

WAR DIARY
or
INTELLIGENCE SUMMARY.
(Erase heading not required.)

Instructions regarding War Diaries and Intelligence Summaries are contained in F. S. Regs., Part II. and the Staff Manual respectively. Title pages will be prepared in manuscript.

Place	Date	Hour	Summary of Events and Information	Remarks and references to Appendices
MAILLY WOOD	16/8/16		Commenced reorganising Coy. & training. Friday bathing parties up to 500 men. Draft of 11 other ranks.	Casualties - Nil
-do-	17/8/16		Training continued – chiefly Bayonet Fighting & specialist's work – in view of future operations. Casualties - N.C. 2/Lt J.E.B. MAUNSELL joined Bn. & posted to Y Coy. 2/Lt T.ROXBY taken on strength & shown on B. Command while employed with 88/1 T.M. Battery.	#2 - 1082 #4 - 1080
-do-	18/8/16		Training continued. 2/Lt W. BRUCE evacuated to England (Wounded)	Other Casualties - Nil #3 - 1073
-do-	19/8/16		Orders to relieve 2nd Royal Fusiliers in Front-Line. Relief completed by 16.30.	Casualties - Nil #3 - 1073
FIRING LINE	20/8/16		Weather beautifully fine (first time during our several tours). Working on Front-Line, F STREET & 2nd AVENUE. Chiefly deepening & widening.	Casualties - 4 O.R. #3 - 1068
AUCHONVILLERS	21/8/16		W & Y Coy moved down to ACHEUX. Work continued. Lt W.S. CAMERON joined Bn. & posted to W Coy.	-do- 3 O.R. Killed #4 - 1061
-do-	22/8/16		-do-	Nil #4 - 1060
-do-	23/8/16		Relieved by Seaforth Bn. of 4th Royal Fusiliers & moved down to ACHEUX. Relief complete by 18.00. Lt C.A. COPLAND invalided (sick) to England. R.S.M. Smith received his Commission & transferred to 9/R.D.F.	#5 - 1067 Draft of 14 Approved Casualties - Nil
ACHEUX	24/8/16		Day given to Salvaging, Cleaning of Equipt. & Kleaning & practising attack.	-do- #3 - 1067
-do-	25/8/16		Training & practising the attack.	-do- #3 - 1066
-do-	26/8/16		-do-	Tomorrow
-do-	27/8/16		-do- ROTTEN ROW, NEW RD, BDWAY, ready for Attack.	Orders to move up to allotted position in 88th TM TRENCH & 1st ESSEX ST. #3 - 1066 Our preparations & arrangements complete.

WAR DIARY or INTELLIGENCE SUMMARY

Army Form C. 2118.

Place	Date	Hour	Summary of Events and Information	Remarks and references to Appendices
ACHEUX	28/6/16		Attack postponed. Intend to make a Raid on German Trenches tonight - or early in morning. Party 43. 1065 of 2 Officers & 80 O'Ranks. Cunningham M16	43 - 1065
-do-	29/6/16		Raiding Party reached Trenches at 0030 - Lt. R.G.G. CUNNINGHAME. 2/Lt J.C DEVOY and 80 O'Ranks. 2/Lt DEVOY laid out tapes to ensure line before our Barrage Lifted but was wounded whilst so doing. 2/Lt J.L.W. FAZAN took his place. Party left our trenches at 0130. When nearing enemy wire line fronted by enemy with bombs, rifle & machine rifles. M. Guns, & T. Mortars & party had to return. All ranks behaved very well and some behaved very gallantly in bringing in dead & wounded. Casualties 3 O.R. killed, 2 officers (Lt. Gun. CUNNINGHAME & 2/Lt. DEVOY) & 7 O'Ranks wounded & 14 O'Ranks missing - but not yet struck off strength.	43 - 1063
-do-	30/6/16		Orders to move up tonight ready for the attack. 6 O'Ranks missing from Raid on came in early on the morning having hidden in shell-holes in "NO MAN'S LAND" all yesterday. Lt McCORMICK rejoined from Staff. Two men of ration party reported missing now reported killed. B. Left ACHEUX at 2300. in following order. - Lewis gun Detachment. B. H.Q. W. X. Z. & Y. Coys. Formed on B. L. MAILLY WOOD & went forward from there by Platoon.	43 - 1061

J.Walker Capt
for Lt Col Duckson
2/7/16

FIFTY SEC...).
Bde. Diar...
156th Inf...

Operation Order
No. 1 by
Capt. A.P. Trimona
Comdg. 1st Royal Dublin Fusiliers
2nd May 1916.

P Map 5/70 40000

1. When the Brigade is in Corps Reserve at LOUVENCOURT it will occupy in case of a general attack the section shown on attached sketch.

2. Section A — 1st Lancs. Fus.
   Section B — 1st Royal Dublin Fus.
   Section C — 2nd Royal Fus. & 1 Middlesex.

3. Starting Point. The Batt... will fall in in column of route on the LOUVENCOURT – ACHEUX Road, the head of the column to be on the junction of the LEALVILLIER & ACHEUX roads.

4. The order of march will be W, X, Y, Z.

5. An advance guard of one officer & one platoon to be detailed by O/C "W" Coy.

(a) Assltg parties 2 coys

Operation Order No 1 (cont'd)

6. Route will be ACHEUX-FORCEVILLE road junction P21 a 54.

7. The Bn. will occupy a front of about 600 yds. Order of position from the right will be W X Y.

8. Z Coy & 3 Lewis machine guns will be in reserve on the road in rear of the line marked brown in sketch.

9. The Lewis machine Gun officer will detail one gun to accompany W X & Y.

10. Ammunition. A reserve of 40 boxes will be established on the road occupied by the reserve coy.

11. A dressing station will be selected by the M.O. in rear of Z Coy.

12. Rear party consisting of the Q.M. and one man per Coy. will remain behind and take charge

Operation Order No 1 (Contd)

of all stores.

13. Only tactical vehicles will proceed with the Battn.

Lieut
9 Adjt. 1/KOYLI

A copy of the sketch herein referred to may be seen at Bn. Orderly Room.

86th BRIGADE EXERCISE　　　　　　Copy No. 4

Ref. sheet 57 B　1/40,000　　　　　　　　　Louvencourt
　　　　　　　　　　　　　　　　　　　　　3 - 5 -16

1. The BRIGADE will route march to-morrow May 4th, via MARIEUX, THIEVRES, AUTHIE.
   Leading Battalion pass Starting Point - Road Junction I 34 A62 at 0900.

2. ORDER OF MARCH :-
   16th MIDDLESEX REGIMENT
   1st LANCASHIRE FUSILIERS
   2nd ROYAL FUSILIERS
   1st ROYAL DUBLIN FUSILIERS.

3. 1st LINE TRANSPORT will march in rear of its respective Battalions.

4. BATTALIONS will detail 1 Officer and 2 N.C.O's to march in rear of the column and bring in stragglers in a formed body. *Parade 8. 45.*
   Starting pt ... I 26 ~~BT 35~~ C 8 9

5. WATCHES will be synchronised 0800 the 4th inst.

6. The following SPECIALIST CLASSES will NOT attend:-
   Wiring & Revetting
   Brigade Grenadier Company
   Bayonet Fighting
   Gas
   Range Party of 16th Middlesex and 1st Royal Dublin Fusiliers.

7. PACKS will be carried.

Issued at 1300
　　　　　　　　　　　　　　　　　　　　Ian Grant
　　　　　　　　　　　　　　　　　　　　Capt.,
　　　　　　　　　　　　　　　Brigade Major, 86th Bde.

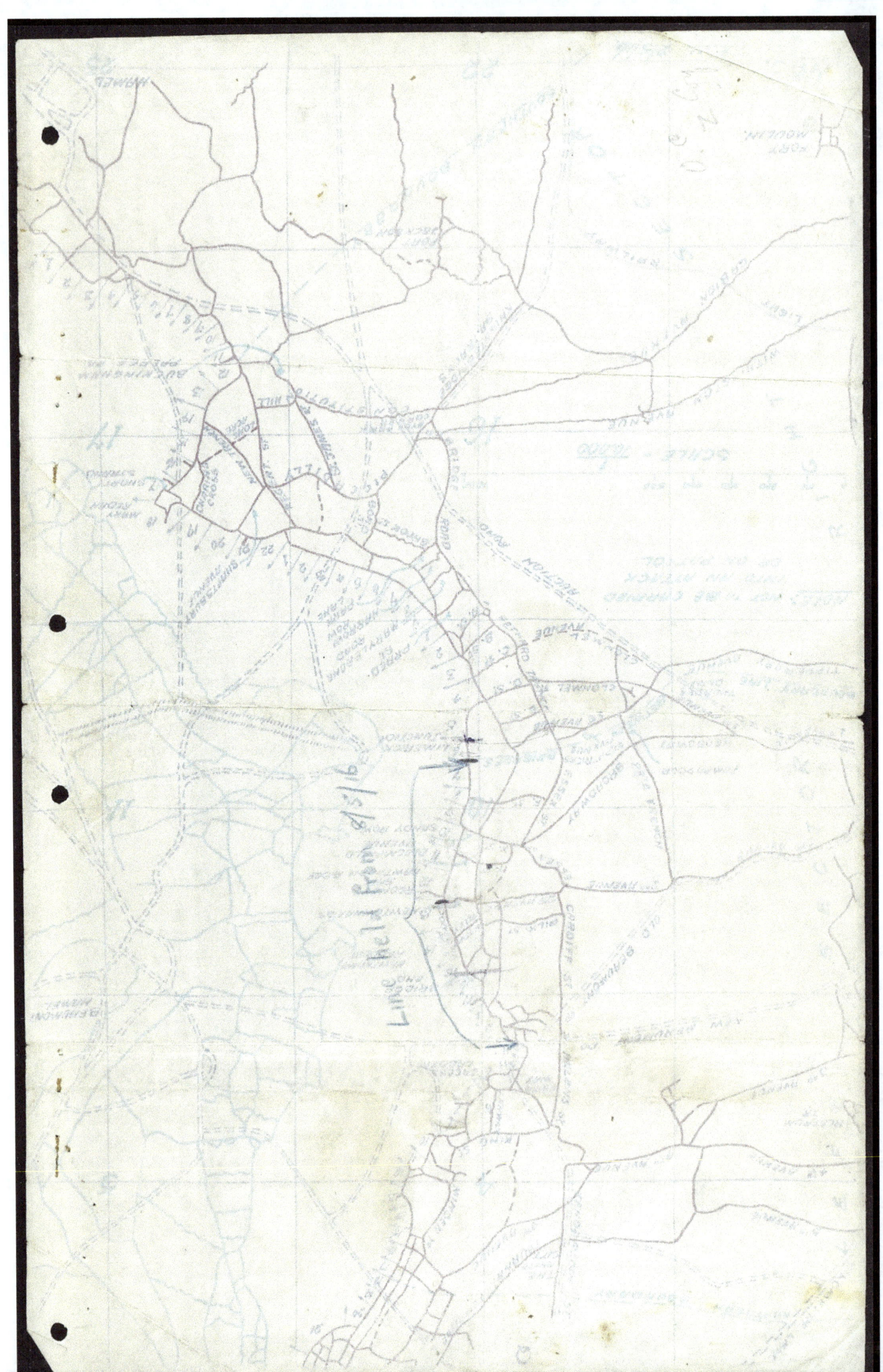

To Ta as 4 PM
Leer 4·10
St (St Deans 4·30

SPECIFIC ORDER   NO 2.

by

Lieut. Col. H. Nelson. D.S.O.

Commanding 1/Royal Dublin Fusiliers.

Monday, 8th May 1916.

MOVE *Coys. will move under*

1. Company arrangements at the times already arranged with Company Commanders.

2. TRANSPORT. Each vehicle, or party of vehicles leaving LOUVENCOURT must be under the charge of an N.C.O. No man is permitted to ride in any vehicle except the driver thereof. Nor may any rifles, equipment or packs be carried on the vehicle except those belonging to the driver. This applies to 1st and 2nd line Transport.

3. Six Headquarter Orderlies will remain with Head Quarters.

4. DRESS. Marching Order. Ground Sheet Blanket and Overcoat to be rolled banderoll fashion, and carried over the right shoulder and under the left arm. Packs, with a list of contents inside, and a duplicate list to be handed to the Quartermaster in accordance with his arrangements.

5. TRENCH STORES. The Regimental Sgt. Major will take over the Bn. Stores, procuring and obtaining receipt for same, and each Coy. will take over Coy. Dumps (including Trench Stores, Tools etc.) They will hand over to the Regimental Sgt. Major, before 0600 tomorrow their respective receipts or copies of same.

6. HEADQUARTERS. Sgt. Geraghty will act as C.Q.M.S. of Head-Quarter Coy. Machine Gun Teams will be rationed by the Coy. with whom they are stationed. Two teams will be rationed with Headquarters. Regimental Signallers will be rationed with Headquarters. Ten to be employed as Orderlies, and six and the Sgt. as Signallers. All other Signallers with their Coys.

7. STRETCHER BEARERS. Two with each Coy. remaining ten with Headquarters. Police, with Hd.Qrs., and act as Ammunition Carriers. Pioneers. two with each Company, and two and the Sgt. with HdQrs. Sanitary Squad. Two with each Coy, and Cpl. with HdQrs. Bombers, with their respective Coys.

                                                           Lieut.

                                          A/Adjt. 1/R.D.Fus.

Reg.Piper will be attached to HdQrs and remain with the Signallers. Snipers of Coys. in front line will be with their Coys. but under supervision of Reg. S.O. Snipers of Reserve Coys. are rationed with HdQrs and will live in a trench to be selected by the S.O. Transport and Grooms will be under the orders of QrMr and will live where he directs.

                                                               P.T.O.

Inspection of Billets.

2/Lt.D.R.Warner will remain behind and inspect billets, and will report to the Adjt. in writing on the condition of same. He will also report to the Staff Captain, and, if necessary, accompany him on his rounds.

TY SECOND DIV.   DARDANELLES.   JUNE 28th 1915(contd).

3.(contd.)
          all men of 156th Bde to sppt trench, over 200 being collected.
          Then moving back to Kink where m.g.s of Bde were B.M. found
          them keeping down fire on portions of H 12 & H 12 A on L held
          by 4/1st and by 7/1st and 7/26th further to R.

          B.M. then retrnd to B.H.Q. and abt 8pm learnt that portions of
          Bde were to be withdrawn from trenches captrd.

          Heaviest cas. were incurred by 8/26th who were enfiladed from
          R by rifles and m.g. fire from abt H 13 A, very few ever reach-
          ing E portion of H 12.   All offs. who reached and occpd H 12
          or H 12 A reported trenches undamaged by our shell-fire & v few
          T dead in them.

          Effective strength:-
                           K   W
          &   872   4/1st.   5 & 61   8 & 61   9 & 141=22 & 345   (4 & 527)
          &   449   7/1st.   4 & 10   3 & 69   4 & 131=11 & 210   (7 & 239)
          &   752   7/26th. 1 & 28   5 & 93   8 & 147=14 & 268   (12 & 484)
          &   653   8/26th. 2 & 28   11 & 114   11 & 306=24 & 448   (1 & 205)
          & 2726.   12 & 127 27 & 419   32 & 725.71 & 1271   24 & 1455.
                                                                1
                                                         72 & 1271(Gen.S-Moncrieff)

                                                           (7/26th).
    Branch. Additional informn supplied.   Lt.Col.Wilson and Adjt are M
             Maj.Findlay comdg 8/26th W.   1st Low.Fd.Amb. arrived.

    4th C of Glasgow Bty R.F.A.   Combined art. shoot from 9am - 10.58am;
             observing from GURKHA BLUFF, from wh inf. had been withdrawn.
             11am guns turned on to H 14.   T trenches badly smashed and
             m.g. redoubt in NULLAH blown to pieces. Bty did not fire dur-
             ing afternoon.

Bde. Diary.
155th Inf.   Advance by Twenty-ninth Div. and 156th Bde took place. Bde
             in Corps Res.

4/21st.   Standing by all day. Twenty-ninth Div. attckg on extreme L
             flank, taking J 10 and 13 and part of H 11 and 12.

5/21st   At CLAPHAM JCTN.

4/25th.   Resting preparatory to attack.

5/25th.   Notice of attack by 155th Bde on 30th recvd.

Bde. Diary.
156th Inf.   Summary of Bde. Orders 27th. Rfce Trench Diagram No. 3.
             NOTE. On a smaller map made by Bde and on a correction of Map
             No. 3, it would appear that a trench had been dug in a westerly
             direction connecting H 12 A and the part of H 11 to the E of
             the ravine.
             (1) Front to be attckd H 12 A,12, 11 and Ravine N.E. of H 11.
             (2) Bde front - Jctn with H 12 to the TURKEY TRENCH.
             (3) Bns. front - 8/26th on R for 300 yds with sppt & res.trenche
                 behind. 7/1st on C for 150 yds   do   do   do   do
                 do.   4/1st " L to the T.T.
                                                                   7/26th.

                                         P.T.O.

OPERATION ORDERS No. 3
by
Lieut. Col H. Nelson, D.S.O.
Commanding 1st Royal Dublin Fusiliers
Wednesday 17th May 1916.
----

1. The Battalion will be relieved by the 2nd Royal Fusiliers tomorrow afternoon the whole relief being completed before dark. In moving between AUCHONVILLERS and MAILLY, no more than a platoon at the most will go in one body and a distance of at least 200 yds must be left between parties. O.Cs Coys and Specialists will make their own arrangements with the officers relieving them subject to the following;-
   (a) At 1400 the relieving Bombers, Lewis Machine Gun Detachment and Snipers will leave MAILLY and come into the trenches by way of 2nd AVENUE.
   (b) At 1500 Y Coy 2nd Royal Fusiliers leaves MAILLY and enters the trenches by way of BROADWAY AVENUE to relieve Z Coy of this Battalion.
   (c) X Coy Royal Fusiliers will leave MAILLY and enter the trenches by way of 2nd AVENUE to relieve W Coy of this Bn.
   (d) At 1700 W Coy 2nd Royal Fusiliers leaves MAILLY and enters the trenches by way of 2nd AVENUE to relieve Y Coy. of this Battalion.
   (e) At 1800 Headquarters party 2nd Royal Fusiliers leaves MAILLY and enters the trenches by way of 2nd AVENUE.
   (f) At 1830 Z Coy 2nd Royal Fusiliers leaves MAILLY and will relieve X Coy at AUCHONVILLERS.

2. O.Cs Coys will report personally to the Adjutant at Bn.Hqrs when their respective reliefs are completed. O.C. X Coy will report by wire.

3. O.Cs Coys will report in writing that their trenches and dugouts are clean and their latrines and sumps in a thoroughly sanitary condition, and that no trench stores are lying anywhere but in their Coy. Dumps.

4. O.Cs Coys and Specialists will please arrange that the duplicate receipt, duly signed, for all trench stores(including picks, shovels and trench boots) is handed in to the Regimental Sgt. Major by 2100 tomorrow.

5. Very Pistols, Periscopes and Wire cutters are not trench stores and will be kept on charge by Companies.

6. Blankets and Greatcoats will be rolled inside the Groundsheet, and carried banderoll fashion over the right shoulder and under the left arm .

7. Lt.R.G.A.Gun Cunningham will act as Baggage Officer and be responsible for the despatch of all Regimental Stores from AUCHONVILLERS. O.C.X Coy. will please detail Baggage Party of 1 sgt and 10 men to report to Lt. R.G.A.Gun Cunningham at 1800.

8. The Quartermaster will act as Billeting Officer, and Coys. will make their own arrangements re guides.

9. While the Battalion is at MAILLY HQrs will consist of the following;-
   Regimental Signallers 17
   HDQR. Orderlies................ 6
   "   Officers' Mess.......... 3
   "   "   Svts. 6
   Canteen Employ................ 2
   Regimental Piper.............. 1
   Orderly Room Staff............ 4
   Post Corporal................. 1
   Medical Officer's Orderlies... 2
   Sanitary Corporal............. 1
   Pioneer Sergeant.............. 1
All other Specialists and Employed will be attached to their

Operations.   - 2 -

respective Companies for Billeting and Rations.

All men undergoing detention or field punishment will be handed over by their Companies to the Provost Sergeant on arrival at MAILLY, and the whole party will be rationed by HQrs.

(Sgd) F.A.Wilson, Lieut. & A/Adjt.

1st Royal Dublin Fusrs.

OPERATION ORDERS No. 4.
by
Lieut. Col. H. Nelson, D.S.O.
Commanding 1st Royal Dublin Fusiliers,
Thursday 18th May 1916.

In the event of an attack the Battalion will take up the following position, (occupying the Green Line).

1. "Y" Coy. will occupy the Green Line from the Railway on the left to, and including, the MAILLY-AUCHONVILLERS ROAD on the right.

2. "Z" Coy. will occupy the Green Line from the right of "Y" Coy. to the short cut from MAILLY to AUCHONVILLERS. (The short cut leaves the MAILLY-ENGLEBELMER ROAD at the Town Control Post.)

3. "X" Coy. will occupy the green line from the right of "Z" Coy. to the Orchard on the north of the MAILLY-ENGLEBELMER ROAD.

4. "W" Coy. will be in reserve on the open space west of MAILLY CHURCH.

The Machine Gun Officer will place six guns in the front line and two with the reserve.

Headquarters will be in its present position.

The Dressing Station will be in its present position.

O's C. Coys. in the front line will take all available Officers and N.C.O's tomorrow morning to inspect the lines to be held by their respective Companies and make their dispositions, and will forward a sketch of their respective portions of the line, with their dispositions, by noon tomorrow.

The accompanying sketches are for your own information. Please make a rough sketch and pass on to the next Coy. Last Coy. to return.

The Commanding Officer will be round the lines in the morning and may be consulted there by any Officer wishing to do so.

(Sgd) F.A.Wilson.
Lieut. & A/Adjt.
1st R.D.F.

OPERATION ORDERS No. 4.
by
Lieut. Col. H. Nelson, D.S.O.
Commanding 1st Royal Dublin Fusiliers,
Saturday 27th May 1916.

In the Field.

1. The Battalion will move to LOUVENCOURT tomorrow evening, upon relief by the Newfoundland Regt. The move will take place under company arrangements.

2. The Battalion will move by platoons, with at least 200 yds. interval, in the following order:-
   "W" Company
   "X"   "
   "Y"   "
   "Z"   "
   Provost Party, and Prisoners.

3. A guide (already arranged for) will meet each company at the cross-roads at the entrance to LOUVENCOURT.

4. All Company Stores and Officers' Kits will be at the Quartermaster's Stores by 0900 tomorrow.

5. Headquarter Company will consist of the same personnel as at MAILLY. All other employed and specialists, except Transport, Grooms, Quartermaster's Staff, Police and Prisoners, will be with their respective companies.

6. O.C. Coys. will report in writing to the Adjutant, on arrival at LOUVENCOURT, when their respective companies are in billets.

7. O.C. Coys. will render the usual certificate in writing to the Adjutant, before leaving MAILLY, that their respective billets are left in a clean and sanitary condition.

8. Lieut. Caldbeck will inspect billets vacated by the companies, report to the Staff Captain, and, if necessary, accompany him on his tour of inspection of the billets.

9. Lieut. Elphick and two N.C.Os to be detailed by O.C. "W" Coy. will march in rear of the provost party, and will bring in to LOUVENCOURT, in a formed body, any stragglers who may fall out during the march.

Lieut. & A/Adjt.
1st R.D.F.

SECRET.

86TH BRIGADE PRELIMINARY OPERATION ORDER.

for training purposes only.

1. The Brigade is to take part in an attack on the German positions. Other Divisions will be attacking on both our flanks for a distance of some miles.

2. The area assigned to the Brigade is as follows:-
   N.BOUNDARY. Q.5.C.2-8- to Q.6.C.5.4.
   S.BOUNDARY. Q.10.D.6.8. to Q.12.B.7.5.

3. The 87th Brigade will be attacking on our right, and the Xth Brigade Yth Division on our left.

4. The attack will commence by a bombardment continuous for 96 hours day and night, up to the moment of the Infantry assault on the 5th day.

5. Further details as to actual date and hour of assault will be issued later.

6. The attack of the Brigade must be pushed home to the fullest extent of our power.

7. During the bombardment the trenches available for the accommodation of the Brigade are:-

    All trenches in front of and including 88th and 86th trenches, North of 1ST AVENUE and South of 4TH AVENUE, as far East as the TENDERLOIN, thence along a line due East to Q.4.D.3.9.5.

    These are allotted to Battalions as follows:-
    2nd Royal Fusiliers in fire and support trenches (including CRIPPS' CUT) South of BRIDGE END.

    1st Lancashire Fusiliers in fire and support trenches (including ST. HELENS) North of BRIDGE END.

-2-

1st R.Dublin Fusiliers -
ESSEX and 88TH TRENCH.

16th Middlesex Regiment CARDIFF and 88TH TRENCH South of NEW BEAUMONT ROAD.

8. The objectives allotted to Battalions for attack are as follows:-

<u>2nd Royal Fusiliers.</u>
German first line system of trenches as far East as STATION ROAD from our Southern Boundary to the NEW BEAUMONT ROAD (exclusive). S.p N of HAWTHORN RED, along C.T running E.

<u>1st Lancashire Fusiliers.</u>
German first line system as far East as WAGON ROAD from NEW BEAUMONT ROAD (inclusive) to our Northern Boundary.

<u>1st R.Dublin Fusiliers.</u>
German second line (BEAUCOURT ROAD) from our Southern Boundary to and including the Communication Trench running S.W. from O of BEAUCOURT ROAD.

<u>16th Middlesex Regiment.</u>
German second line (BEAUCOURT ROAD) from above mentioned Communication Trench (exclusive) to our Northern Boundary.

9. On the morning of the assault troops of the Brigade will be formed up in their trenches opposite their areas of attack.

The hour and full details as to the route each company is to move by will be considered by the Commanding Officers concerned.

10. The following details will be attached to Battalions:-

<u>2nd Royal Fusiliers.</u> 2 Vickers Maxim guns.
1 section R.E.
1 ~~bombing company.~~

1st Lancashire Fusrs) 2 Vickers Maxim guns
1st R.Dublin Fusrs.) 1 section R.E.
16th Middlesex Regt.)

11. (a) The two leading battalions will deliver their assault with each two companies in first line, two companies in battalion reserve.

-2-

Companies will assault, in depth, on a frontage of one platoon.

(b) Their tasks will be :-

2nd Royal Fusrs.
To move straight forward to their ultimate objective detaching bombing company to protect their left flank, by holding the communication trench running along south side of BEAUMONT HAMEL road and bombing up and blocking all approaches to that trench from the village.

1st Lancashire Fusiliers.
To move forward and establish themselves in the enemy trenches immediately West of BEAUMONT HAMEL and systematically bomb up and block all communication trenches leading to that village for a distance of 40 yards.

(c) The leading companies will NOT occupy and consolidate positions won until they reach their final objective - they must push on.

(d) The 4th company in each battalion, or two platoons of each 3rd and 4th Company will be detailed to

  (a) consolidate.
  (b) deal with prisoners.
  (c) bomb deep dug outs.

Strong points for consolidation will, as far as possible, be previously decided on, but it must be understood that with the "man on the spot" rests the real decision as to these places.

(e) During assault each platoon will move at once forward into the place of the platoon immediately to its front - communication trenches will not be used. Troops must move across the open.

12. EQUIPMENT.

 (a) Packs will be left behind in our own trenches; all ranks carry two waterbottles.
 (b) Infantry of assaulting columns:-
  120 rounds S.A.A., 2 sandbags in belt, 2 Mills grenades, 10 wirecutters per platoon and hedging gloves, 2 trench bridges per platoon, a shovel or pick (one pick to 5 shovels)

(c) Infantry of consolidating parties:-
200 rounds S.A.A., shovel or pick (one pick to 3 shovels) 25 sandbags. Wiring party of 12 to carry, each a wire-cutter, pair hedging gloves, roll of barbed wire and 2 mauls to the party.

(d) Grenadiers.
One man in two only slung rifle and 50 rounds S.A.A. 12 grenades. Carriers each carry 2 buckets full of grenades.

(e) Lewis gunners:-
25% carry rifles and 120 rounds S.A.A.

(f) Light Trench Mortar gunners:-
25% carry rifles and 120 rounds S.A.A.

(g) Signallers:-
Rifle and 120 rounds.

(h) Stretcher bearers:-
Belt braces and medical haversack.

(i) Runners:-
Dressed in shorts; rifle and 50 rounds S.A.A.

13. All ranks will wear gas helmets rolled up under their steel helmets ready to be lowered immediately in case of gas.

14. The 2nd Royal Fusiliers and 1st Lancashire Fusiliers will cut passages through our wire every night during the bombardment. Places where wire is cut will be marked in the trench immediately opposite.

15. During the nights of bombardment the Machine Gun Company will fire on the enemy wire in short bursts throughout the night.

16. As soon as the leading columns of assault are in the enemy trenches, the Stokes Gun Batteries will push forward to positions to be indicated.

Battery Commander will send in a report today shewing number of men required to help him move his guns and ammunition forward.

17. The two battalions in Brigade reserve entrusted with the capture of the German second line will move up into the

fire and support trenches opposite their objectives as soon as these are vacated. Battalion Commanders will consider the routes to be used by their companies.

18. As soon as the leading battalions are clear of our trenches, the reserve battalions will prepare for their advance.

(a) Their advance will be proceded by small advanced guards and will be by bounds, the battalion being re-organized after each bound preparatory to further advance.

First bound STATION ROAD.
Second "   safe to edge of dead ground towards enemy trench.

(b) Formation. Each company in diamond formation, two companies front line, two companies battalion reserve, or each company in diamond formation and the battalion ditto, i.e.

"A Company"

```
              No.1 Platoon
                  ↑
   No2 ←—50ˣ—→ ↑ ←—50ˣ—→ No 3
        ←————250ˣ————→
                  ↓
                No 4
```

19. Battalions will organize a system of runners to keep touch between their own companies and their Headquarters.

20. The following Dressing Stations will be established:-
    Advanced Dressing Station:-

    (1) TENDERLOIN.
    (2) Present Headquarters of right battalion in
        our line.

21. Our own wounded must be left alone by our men. On no account are men to fall out to attend to them.

22. No looting is to be allowed. This is a Court Martial offence, for which the punishment is "to be shot".

These orders are by no means complete. They are for practice only, to enable Battalion Commanders to think out the various problems that will arise should an attack be ordered.

On Saturday next this exercise will be carried out as near as possible according to these orders, on the Brigade Training Ground. In the meantime Commanding Officers are requested to rehearse their special parts of it.

31-5-16

Y Coy ZM.
W Coy WR

Orders by Lt. Colonel Nelson,
Commanding 1st R.D.F.
                                    "Quartermasters Dept."

1. Transport will be available at Auchonville at 8 p.m. as follows::
Officers Mess Cart to be at head of 2nd Avenue, for Head Quarter Mess
and material. One G.S.Limber will be in a similar position, This
Limber is allotted for Orderly Room, ~~and the Baggage of~~
   One G.S.Limber will be in a similar position for the kits of
the Officers of Head Quarters.
   3 Limbers will be on the right of the road facing towards Mailly
near to where the Battalion Cookers are. These limbers are allotted
one per company. The first limber is allotted for "Y" Co. the
second for W.Co., and the third for Z. Co.
   One limbered G.S. Wagon is allotted for X Co. and will be
in position in the yard outside the Officers Mess.
   The Maltese Cart will be in position at the rear of the
third Company Limber, near to the 2nd Avenue, but not on it. The
top of this avenue is reserved for vehicles for Head Quarter Mess,
baggage and Orderly Room. Each vehicle ~~will be~~ on this 2nd Avenue
road will be backed down the road as far as possible. They will be
in line, and on the right of the road in the following order
coming from the communication trench
   1 Limbered G.S. Wagon for Head Quarter Officers Kit.
   1 Limbered G.S. Wagon for Orderly Room.
   1 Officers Mess Cart.

These three vehicles are preceded by the following vehicles
   1 Maltese Cart.
   1 G.S.Limbered Wagon Z Co.
   1 G.S.Limbered Wagon W Co.
   1 G.S.Limbered Wagon Y Co.
referred to above.
   The two Battalion water carts will be moved at 8 p.m.
and placed in the Yard at the Q.M.Stores.
   The G.S.Limbered Wagon, containing the 20000 rounds of
reserve Ammunition will be moved similarly, and the ammunition
dumped in the Ammunition Store in the Quartermasters Store.
   No vehicle will be moved after its being loaded until
the following has reported to the Transport Sergeant.
   Company Vehicles- The Co. Qr.Mr.Sergeant.
   Maltese Cart. The Medical Officers Corporal.
   Orderly Room Limber- The Orderly Room Sergeant.
   Head Quarter Officers Kit Limber- The Colonels Servant.

Co.   ~~All~~ vehicles as soon as reported ready to move will be taken to
Company Officers billets- where they will be unloaded under Company
arrangements. A servant will accompany each Limber on which Officers
kit is placed. The vehicles for H.Q. will be unloaded under the R.S.M.
   The remaining G.S.Limbers, not allotted, will be in
reserve in the Battalion Yard (where the Water Carts are) at
Auchonville, and will move back to Mailly under the orders of the
Transport Officer.
   Tea will be provided from Company Cookers as soon as the men
are settled in their billets. H.Q. Co. will have tea under arrange-
ments made by the A.Q.M.S. of the Co.
   Kit bags will be withdrawn from the Q.M.Stores by 8 a.m.
on the 18th Inst.
   A Shoemakers and Tailors shop is established in the Q.M.
Stores and will be available for work from 9 a.m. 18/5/ onwards.

OPERATION ORDERS   No. 5.
by
Lieut. Col. H. Watson. D.S.O.
Commanding 1st Royal Dublin Fusiliers.
5th June 1916.

In the Field.

Reference Trench Map "Beaumont".

1. In accordance with Brigade Operation Orders the Battalion will take part in an attack on the German positions, and, with the 16th Middlesex, will be in Brigade reserve.

2. The objective of the Royal Dublin Fusiliers will be the German second line, from, and including, the communication trench running southwest from the "O" in "BEAUCOURT ROAD" southwards to the "D" in "ROAD".

3. The German trenches will be bombarded for 96 hours. On the morning of assault the Battalion will be formed up W and X Coys in front, Y and Z reserve, as follows:-
   W Coy. in ESSEX STREET from its junction with BROADWAY to the south.
   X Coy in ESSEX STREET from its junction with BROADWAY to 2ND AVENUE.
   Y Coy. in 88TH TRENCH, its right on BROADWAY.
   Z Coy. in 88TH TRENCH, its left on 2ND AVENUE.

xxxxxxxxxxxxxxxxxxxxxxxxxxxxxxxxxxxxxxxxxxxxxxxxxxxxxxxxxxxxxxxxxxxxxx
xxxxxxxxxxxxxxxxxxxxxxxxxxxxxxxxxxxxxxxxxxxxxxxxxxxxxxxxxxxxxxxxxxxxxx.

4. Constant touch will be maintained, by means of messengers, between our front companies and the Battalion in front, the Royal Fusiliers, and between our front companies and the companies in 88TH TRENCH. As soon as the Royal Fusiliers commence to evacuate the front trenches, W Coy, moving via F STREET, BROADWAY and BLOOMFIELD, will occupy the front trenches vacated by the Royal Fusiliers, from Bay 11 inclusive to Bay 7 inclusive. At the same time X Coy, moving 2nd AVENUE, HAPPY ALLEY and MCLAREN'S LANE, will occupy the front trenches, vacated by the Royal Fusiliers, from BRIDGE END southwards to Bay 13 inclusive. When W and X Companies are clear of ESSEX STREET, Y Coy, moving via BROADWAY, F STREET and BLOOMFIELD, and Z Coy, moving via 2nd AVENUE, Happy Alley and MCLAREN'S LANE, will be prepared to occupy the front trenches vacated by W and X companies respectively.

5. The first bound will be to STATION ROAD. In this advance the battalion will move in depth on a frontage of 2 companies in line of platoons in platoon column, in file, with 50 yds interval, and 50 yds distance between sections. The left section of W company will direct, marching on a bearing of 100 degrees. The leading companies will be preceded by small advanced guards.
On reaching STATION ROAD companies will close on the front, reorganise, and prepare for the next bound, the right of W company being 50 yds. north of the CEMETERY, and the left of X 100 yds. south of the CHURCH, BEAUMONT, a covering party being sent out by W and X companies.

6. The second bound will be from STATION ROAD to the dead ground southeast, where the battalion will form for assault. 7. The assault will be delivered by the battalion on a front of 2 companies in line of platoons in platoon column, and in extended order, W and X in front, Y and Z in reserve. The right of W company will advance on the "B" in "BEAUCOURT ROAD", and the left of X on the "O" in "BEAUCOURT ROAD". Each company will ensure that the flow is properly maintained, sections

Operation Orders No. 5.   -2-

spring into the place of the one directly in front, directly the latter moves on.

8. Bombing squads will move on the outer platoons of companies.

9. The O.C. Machine Gun Section will move in the rear of the rear platoon of Y Company. During the assault he will take up a position in or near STATION ROAD, and be prepared to assist the advance of the Battalion, particularly watching the left flank.

10. Equipment. (a) Packs will be left behind in our own trenches. All ranks carry two water bottles. The haversack will be carried on the back. Every man will carry either a pick or a shovel, placed handle downwards between the brace and body, on the back. Front companies carry one pick to five shovels, reserve companies one pick to three shovels.
  (b) W, X and Y companies will carry 120 rounds S.A.A. two sandbags in belt, two Mills Grenades, 10 wirecutters per platoon, hedging gloves, two trench   per platoon.
  (c) Z company will carry 200 rounds S.A.A. 25 sandbags. This company will detail a Wiring Party of 12 men, each to carry a wirecutter, pair of hedging gloves, roll of barbed wire, and two mauls to the party.
  (d) Grenadiers. One man in two sling rifles
    Carriers each carry two buckets full of grenades.
  (e) Lewis Gunners. 25% carry rifles and 120 rounds S.A.A.
  (f) Signallers. Rifle and 120 rounds.
  (g) Stretcher Bearers. No rifles or ammunition.
  (h) Runners. Rifle and one bandolier.

11. All ranks will wear Gas Helmets under their Steel Helmets, ready for wearing if required.

12. Dressing Station will be as at present.

13. No man is to fall out to attend to the wounded.

14. The punishment for looting is "To be shot".

15. O.C. Z Company will arrange for the custody of all prisoners, and their despatch to the rear

16. Battalion Headquarters will be in 26th TRENCH during the bombardment. When the Battalion is at STATION ROAD it will be in HAWTHORN REDOUBT, and when the Battalion is in BEAUCOURT ROAD the Battalion Headquarters will be in STATION ROAD.

17. After capturing the BEAUCOURT ROAD, flank companies will immediately send strong bombing parties along the trench to their flank to open up communications with the 87th Brigade on our right, and the 16th Middlesex on our left.

18. A few scouts and a covering party will be sent out by Z company at dusk and small parties should be sent by each company to collect ammunition, water bottles and iron rations from casualties in the vicinity.

Operation Orders No. 5.   - 3 -

19. Captured rifles and ammunition must be carefully collected and made use of in case our own rifles are damaged.

20. The captured line is to be held at all costs, and every effort made to render it impregnable.

21. The Machine Gun officer will detail four Lewis Machine Guns to each company.

22. Two days iron rations will be carried by all ranks.

[signature]

Lieut. & A/Adjt.
1st R.D.F.

OPERATION ORDERS
by
Lieut. Col. H. Nelson, D.S.O.
Commanding 1st Royal Dublin Fusiliers,
Tuesday 6th June, 1916.

No. 6.

1. The Battalion will move into the trenches tomorrow afternoon, and relieve the 1st Essex Regt. on the right of the left sector.

2. Companies will march to ACHEUX WOOD independently, in the following order:- (W Company to move at 1300)
   Headquarters,
   "W" Company
   "X"   "
   "Y"   "
   "Z"   "

From ACHEUX WOOD they will proceed by platoons, at least 200 yds. distance between platoons.

3. "W" Company will take over the right of the line and will move in via BROADWAY.

4. "X" Company will take over the left of the line, and will move in by way of 2ND AVENUE.

5. "Z" Company will be in support, in 88TH TRENCH, and will move in by way of 2ND AVENUE.

6. "Y" Company will be in reserve in AUCHONVILLERS.

7. O.C. Companies, with their respective Sgt. Majors, the Reg. Sgt. Major, and officers in charge of Lewis Machine Gun Section, Signallers, Bombers, Intelligence and Sniping, will proceed to the trenches tomorrow morning to arrange details, take over stores etc. A proportion of Machine Gunners, Signallers and Snipers will go with this party. The usual receipts will be taken and given for all trench stores, and a duplicate of such receipt forwarded to the Adjutant by 1800 tomorrow.

8. O.C. Coys. will render the usual certificate to the Adjutant that billets have been left in a clean and sanitary condition.

9. Immediately the relief is completed O.C. Coys. will report to the Adjutant by wire or by messenger.

10. 2/Lt. H.V. Spankie will inspect all billets after the departure of the Battalion, will report to the Staff Captain, and, if necessary, accompany him round the billets.

11. 2/Lt. C.F. Greenlees, and two N.C.Os, to be detailed by O.C. "Y" Coy., will march in rear of the Battalion, and bring to Battalion Headquarters, in a formed body, any men who fall out from the line of march.

12. TRANSPORT. LT. C.B. Davis will act as Transport Officer for the move.

(a) Coy. Stores. One G.S. limbered wagon is allotted to each Company, and will be at Company Headquarters at 1300. All Company Stores, Officers Kit and Mess Kit, will be loaded on this wagon.

(b) Orderly Room. One G.S. limbered wagon is allotted to Headquarter Officers' kit, and Orderly Room stores, and will be at Battalion Headquarters at 1300.

(c) Canteen. One G.S. limbered wagon is allotted to the Regimental-Canteen, and will be outside Headquarters Officers'

Operation Orders.   No. 6.

- 2 -

Mess at 1300.

(d) The maltese cart and mess cart will be available for Medical Stores and Headquarter Officers' Mess Stores respectively, and will be in position ready for loading at 1300.

(e) <u>General</u>. All vehicles with stores for the trenches will halt outside MAILLEY CHURCH until dusk, and will move on when ordered to do so by the Transport Officer.

N.C.Os and men marching with the transport will on no account ride on the wagons, nor will anyone place equipment or accoutrements on the wagons, except the drivers.

Wagons will move out in twos, with an N.C.O. in charge of each two.

13. Caps (tied or sewn in sacks) and Blankets (rolled in tens, with a waterproof sheet outside each roll) will be handed in to the Quartermaster's Stores by 0730 tomorrow. Coy. Q.M.Sgts. will accompany the caps and blankets/wagons of their respective Coys., and will personally superintend the storage or removal of same.

14. <u>Headquarters</u>. Headquarters will be composed as under;-

    Signallers................17
    Battalion Orderlies.......5
    Pioneers..................1 (Sgt)
    Sanitary Squad............1 (Cpl)
    Officers' Servants........6
    Headquarter Mess 3
    Orderly Room Staff........4
    Police....................11
    Stretcher Bearers.........2 (M.O's Orderlies)

15. <u>Specialists</u>.
(a) Bombers will be with their respective Coys.
(b) Machine Gunners will be with their respective Coys.
(c) Signallers with their respective companies, except the 17 with Headquarters.
(d) Stretcher Bearers with their respective companies (except the M.O's Orderlies)
(e) Pioneers with their respective companies.
(f) Sanitary Squad with their respective companies.
(g) Snipers will be as a separate party, under the sniping officer, in a portion of the trench to be selected by this officer. They will be attached for rations to the Coy. in whose lines they are.
(h) Raiding Party, will not go into the trenches, but will be billetted in MAILLEY MALLET. The party will march in rear of "Y" Company.
(j) The Regimental Piper will be attached for rations to the Company in reserve at Auchonvillers ("Y" Coy.)

(Sgd.) J.A. Wilson
Lieut. & A/Adjt.
1st R.D.F.

1st ROYAL DUBLIN FUSILIERS.

ORDERS FOR THE MOVE.

1. The Battalion will be relieved by the 2nd Royal Fusiliers this afternoon. O.C. Coys. will make their own detailed arrangements with the Companies relieving them.

2. All Trench Stores will be collected in the various dumps, the usual Inventories XXXXX made, and receipts given and taken, duplicates of such receipts to be in the Orderly Room by 1500. (Very Pistols Periscopes and Wire Cutters will in no case be handed over)

3. Blankets, rolled in bundles of ten, with oilsheets round the outside, Officers' Kits, Coy. and Mess Stores, will be sent down to the light railway near the foot of 2nd AVENUE during the morning. Everything to be down by 2 pm, latest.

4. O.C. Coys. will report to the Adjutant that their lines are left clean. They will also report to the Adjutant upon the relief of their respective Companies being completed.

5. C.Q.M.Sgts. will make themselves acquainted with the distribution of their respective Companies in the Huts at MAILLEY, and will have a sufficient number of guides to meet their Companies upon arrival.

6. All Specialists will be relieved during the morning if possible.

7. Upon return to MAILLEY all Specialists and Employed Men will be with their respective Companies.

8. Headquarters will be composed as at present.

(Sgd.) G.A. Wilson
Lieut. & A/Adjt.
1st R.D.F.

15th June 1916.

OPERATION ORDERS
by
Lieut. Col. H. Nelson, D.S.O.
Commanding 1st Royal Dublin Fusiliers,
17th June 1916.

No. 5.

In the Field.

Reference Trench Map "BEAUMONT" (1 - 10,000)

1. In accordance with Brigade Operation Orders the Battalion will take part in an attack on the German positions, and, with the 16th Middlesex, will be in Brigade Reserve.

2. The objective of the Royal Dublin Fusiliers will be the German second line, from, and including, the communication trench running S.W. from the "O" IN "BEAUCOURT ROAD", Southwards to the "D" in "ROAD".

3. The German trenches will be bombarded for 96 hours. On the morning of assault the Battalion will be formed up, W and X Coys. in front, and Y and Z reserve, as follows:-
   W Coy. in ESSEX STREET from its junction with BROADWAY to the south.
   X -   in ESSEX STREET from its junction with BROADWAY to 2ND AVENUE.
   Y -   in 88TH TRENCH, its right on BROADWAY.
   Z -   in 88TH TRENCH, its left on 2ND AVENUE.

4. Constant touch will be maintained by means of messengers, between the Royal Fusiliers, and between our front and reserve companies.. As soon as the Royal Fusiliers commence to evacuate the front trenches, W Coy., moving via F STREET and BROADWAY, will occupy the front trenches from the mine N to BROADWAY (inclusive), and X Coy., moving via 2ND AVENUE and BLOOMFIELD, will occupy the front trenches from BROADWAY (exclusive) North to ROONEY'S SAP (inclusive). Y Coy. will follow W, and Z Coy. will follow X Coy.

5. In the advance through the enemy's front trenches, the dividing line between the Royal Dublin Fusiliers and the Middlesex Regt., will be from ROONEY's SAP, along communication trench 43 (inclusive) to STATION ROAD. The dividing line between The Dublin Fusiliers and the 87th Brigade will be the mine, Y Ravine (exclusive) to STATION ROAD. STATION ROAD is allotted to the Battalion from point 1432 to a point 200 yds. NW of QUARRY.

6. The first bound will be to STATION ROAD. In this advance the Battalion will move in depth, on a frontage of two companies in line of platoons in platoon column in file, at 45 yds interval and 100 yds distance. The right sections of each line will direct, marching on Y RAVINE. The leading Companies will be preceded by small advanced guards, which will act as a covering party while the Battalion reorganises on STATION ROAD. On reaching STATION ROAD Coys. will close, W Coy. moving South until their right rests on POINT 1432. X Coy. will close to the right until its left is on a point 200 yds. NW of QUARRY. X will follow W, and Z will form up between X and Y. Coys. will reorganise and prepare for the next advance. A bombing party under Lieut.
from X and Z Coys. will at once proceed up STATION ALLEY, and keeping behind our artillery barrage will clear the Germans out of that trench.

7. The advance for the assault will be on a front of two companies, in line of platoons in platoon column in extended order to 5 paces, and 40 yds distance between lines. The right of W Coy. will advance from point 1432 on a bearing of 62 degrees and the left of X on a bearing of 82 degrees, to the junction of STATION ALLEY with BEAUCOURT ROAD. Companies will form up for the advance on the

O.O. No. 5.

sloping ground East of STATION ROAD and clear of it, and the advance will be simultaneous with that of the MIDDLESEX REGT. A few scouts should precede the advance. Bombing squads will move with the outer platoons of Coys. Touch must be maintained with the BORDER REGT. on the right and the MIDDLESEX REGT. on the left. The pace will be quick time until the assault at 20 yds distance. The advance will be covered by our artillery until 1.20 and the advance should be so timed that the assault is made very shortly after the artillery lifts at that hour. The advance must be steady, and O.C. Coys. will ensure that the flow is properly maintained. It may be necessary to halt, both to prevent running into our artillery barrage, and also to enable the rear lines to close up to the front, prior to the assault. The assault should be made in two lines of single rank, at about 50 yds. distance between lines.

8. After taking BEAUCOURT TRENCH, Y Coy. will send bombers down the trenches on their right and open up communication with the BORDER REGT. Y Coy. will send a party down the trench running NE from the "R" in "ROAD". All companies will push forward one section and also one Lewis Gun, as a covering party. Also a few men with wire cutters to cut a passage through the wire between the communication trench running NW and Point 4744. Z Coy. will at once consolidate the junction of STATION ALLEY and BEAUCOURT ROAD, and also the fork at 100 yds. NEast of XXXX junction of BEAUCOURT ROAD with communication trench running NW from it, as strong posts. Y Coy. will consolidate the bend of the right branch of this trench at a point 120 yds. NE of "D" in "ROAD". A Lewis Gun will be in each strong post. Snipers should be sent forward to pick off the enemy artillery. All Companies will consolidate the captured trench, making at least one machine gun emplacement each, sites for Lewis Gun positions should be carefully selected and marked. In case little opposition is met with it will be necessary to dig a trench either in front or in rear of that captured. Orders regarding this will be issued at a later date.

9. Lewis Guns will move on the outer flanks, with the rear section of companies. The O.C. Machine Gun Section will move up STATION ALLEY in rear of the bombing party, and from their positions in the trench assist the advance as circumstances permit. He will select suitable positions in BEAUCOURT ROAD, and cover the advance of the 88th Brigade on XXX PUISIEUX TRENCH.

10. EQUIPMENT. (a) Packs will be left behind in our own trenches. All ranks carry two water bottles. The haversack will be carried on the back. Every man will carry either a pick or a shovel, placed handle downwards between the brace and the body, on the back. Front Coys. carry one pick to five shovels, reserve Coys. one pick to three shovels.
Each man will carry (b) W, X, and Y Coys. will carry 120 rounds S.A.A. 120 rounds of Ammn will be carried two sandbags in belt, two Mills Grenades, 10 Wire Cutters per platoon, hedging gloves, two trench ladders per platoon.
(c) Z Coy. will carry 200 rounds S.A.A., 25 sandbags, and this Coy. will detail a wiring party of 12 men, each to carry a wire cutter, pair of hedging gloves, roll of barbed wire, and two mauls to the party.
(d) Grenadiers. One man in two sling rifles. Carriers each carry two buckets full of Grenades.
(e) Lewis Gunners. 25% carry rifles and 120 rounds S.A.A.
(f) Signallers. Rifle and 120 rounds.
(g) Stretcher Bearers. No rifles or ammunition.
(h) Runners. Rifle and one bandolier.

11. All ranks will wear Gas Helmets under their Steel Helmets, ready for wearing if required.

O.O. No. 5.

- 3 -

12. Dressing Station will be as ~~at present~~.

13. No man is to fall out to attend to the wounded.

14. The punishment for lotting is "To be shot".

15. O.C. Z Coy. will arrange for the custody of all prisoners, and their despatch to the rear.

16. Battalion Headquarters will be in F STREET during the bombardment, and when the Battalion is at STATION ROAD Battalion Headquarters will move by mine and Y RAVINE to QUARRY.

17. A few scouts and a covering party will be sent out by Z Coy. at dusk, and small parties should be sent by each Coy. to collect ammunition, water bottles and iron rations from casualties in the vicinity.

18. Captured rifles and ammunition must be carefully collected and made use of, in case our own rifles are damaged.

19. The captured line is to be held at all costs, and every effort made to render it impregnable.

20. The Machine Gun Officer will detail two Lewis Machine Guns to each Company.

21. One day's iron rations will be carried by all ranks. *as well as the current days one —*

Lieut. & A/Adjt.
1st R.D.F.

SECRET.

B.M.A. 3/17.

O.C. 1st Royal Dublin Fus

Men of the 88th Brigade will wear a triangular Tin disc, with a 2 inch Red streak down the centre in the forthcoming operations.

17/6/1916

Ian Grant
Captain.
Brigade Major, 86th Brigade.

1st Royal Dublin Fusiliers.   18th June 1916.

ORDERS FOR THE MOVE.

The Battalion will take over tomorrow afternoon, the front line trenches at present held by the 2/Royal Fusiliers. "Z" Coy. will take over the right of the line, and "X" Coy. the left. "W" and "Y" Coys. will be in support in AUCHONVILLERS.

1. Coys. will take over by Coy. arrangements, moving up by platoons at at least 200 yds. distance, the route to be the new track, about 500 or 600 yds. east of MAILLEY WOOD, already reconnoitred by Coys.

2. Coys. will move up in the following order, Z, X, W, Y. The leading platoon of "Z" Coy. will move off at 1330. and the leading platoon of "W" Coy. at 1430.

3. O.C.Coys. with their Sgt. Majors, Specialist Officers, with all specialists, and the Regimental Sgt. Major, will proceed to the trenches during the morning, as usual.

4. The usual certificate as to quarters vacated will be rendered to the Adjt., a duplicate receipt for Trench Stores will be sent to Orderly Room by 1500, and all Coys. will report to the Adjt.when the relief is completed. The following Specialist Officers will also report upon their respective reliefs being completed;-
                2/Lt. Pearson....Snipers.
                2/Lt. Hollom.....Lewis Gun.
                2/Lt. Spankie....Bombers.
                2/Lt. Trotter....Signallers.

5. Blankets rolled in bundles of 10, with groundsheets round them, will be sent to the Quartermaster's Stores by 0900 tomorrow.

6. The Transport Officer will arrange that;-
    One limber per Coy. is as near as possible to the Coy. HeadQrs. by 0900.
    One limber as near as possible to Battalion Orderly Room at 1400
    Remainder to be at Quartermaster's Stores at 0900.
    Officers Mess Cart to be as near as possible to Headquarters Officers Mess at 1330.
    The Maltese Cart will be as near as possible tothe Medical Inspection Room at 1100.

7. 2/Lt. Durward will remain behind, inspect huts and lines generally, after the departure of the Battalion, and render a report in writing to the Adjt.

8. 2/Lt. McKenzie, with two N.C.Os to be detailed by O.C. "Y"Coy., will march in rear of the Battalion, and take charge of all stragglers and men who drop out on the line of march. He will render a report in writing to the Adjt.

                                      Lieut. & A/Adjt.
                                      1st R.D.F.

B.M.A. 4/19.   SECRET.

O.C. 1st Bn. R. Dublin Fusiliers.

In the forthcoming offensive operations if heavy Artillery fire is required on any particular locality in in case of emergency, or when a specially favourable target presents itself, the prefix AA followed by the Map square designation of the target will be sent.

This should be used with R.F.C. and Artillery units.

19/6/1916.

Ian Grant
Capt.
Brigade Major, 86th Inf. Bde.

ORDERS FOR THE MOVE,
by
Lieut. Col. H. Nelson, D.S.O.
Commanding 1st Royal Dublin Fusiliers,
Thursday 22nd June, 1916.
In the Field.

The Battalion, less "W" and "Y" Coys. will move to ACHEUX tommorrow afternoon, upon being relieved by the 2nd Royal Fusiliers.

1. The relief will be carried out under company arrangements, the usual certificates and reports being rendered to the Adjutant, by Coy. Commanders.

2. All Periscopes, Very Pistols, Illuminating Pistols and Wire Cutters will be taken. Picks and Shovels will be taken unless the Royal Fusiliers hand over a similar number to the Quartermaster at ACHEUX.

3. Blankets, rolled in bundles of 10, Officers' Kit and Mess Stores will be at the Railway Crossing by 0930 tomorrow.

4. Coys. will march by platoons or half-platoons, at at least 200 yds. distance, via BROADWAY, New Track and ROTTEN ROW.

5. Transport will proceed via ROTTEN ROW if the weather is fine, otherwise by BEAUSSART-BERTRANCOURT, and must be clear of P17 B99 by 1300.

6. Coys. will send on one N.C.O. or man per platoon to guide the Coys. into tents or billets at ACHEUX.

7. Specialists will be relieved, and stores handed over, during the morning.

8. Coys. will detail 10 men per coy to act as loaders. They will also act as escort.

(Sgd) F.A. Wilson,
Lieut. & A/Adjt.
1st R.D.F.

AFTER ORDER No. 873A.
by
Lieut. Col. H. Nelson, D.S.O.
Commanding 1st Royal Dublin Fusiliers,
Tuesday 20th June, 1916.
In the Field.

MOVE. "W" and "Y" Coys. of this Battalion will move to ACHEUX tomorrow afternoon, under Coy. arrangements, the exact time of departure to be notified later.

1. A party of 10 other ranks will report to the Quartermaster at the SUCHERIE, ACHEUX, at 0900, to pitch tents.

11. One G.S. and 2 limbered wagons will be at AUCHONVILLERS Railway Crossing at 1400 for Blabkets and other baggage. Coys. will detail loading parties, who will act as escort also.

111. Two Cookers and one Watercart will be moved to ACHEUX tomorrow night, and meanwhile any necessary cooking at ACHEUX for "W" and "Y" Coys. will be done in camp kettles.

Lieut. & A/Adjt.
1st R.D.F.

S E C R E T.   B.M.A. 4.   23/6/16.

ALL BATTALIONS.

On Y/Z night two Brigade Headquarter Runners will join Battalion Headquarters, these will, ~~be used~~ in the absence or breakdown of Telephonic Communication, be used to keep touch between advanced Battalion Headquarters after their establishment in the German Trenches and Brigade Battle Headquarters.

Battalions must be prepared to supplement these men by their own runners.

                                                            Captain.,
23/6/16.   Brigade Major, 86th Brigade.

Copy No. 6

OPERATION ORDERS
by
Lieut. Col. H. Nelson, D.S.O.
Commanding 1st Royal Dublin Fusiliers.

In the Field.
26th June 1916.

Reference Trench Map BEAUMONT 1/10,000.

1. In the attack on the German lines the objective of the Royal Dublin Fusiliers is BEAUCOURT ROAD TRENCH, from Point 98 (inclusive) to the REDOUBT (exclusive).

2. The Battalion will leave our front trenches in the formation previously laid down, and passing through the Royal Fusiliers will close on the leading line and reorganise on the ground 150 yds. East of STATION ROAD. It is to be clearly understood by all ranks that it is imperative that the advance to this point be carried out without a pause, and the greatest care must be taken not to get mixed up with the Battalion in front. Scouts precede our advance, and are responsible for pointing out where the enemy's trenches can be crossed, and for covering the Battalion whilst reorganising.

3. After reorganising platoons will move to the right across STATION ALLEY, get into position parallel to our objective, and close behind our artillery barrage. Coys. will at once form up for the attack and wait for the barrage to lift at 1.5.

4. At 1.5 the Battalion will advance preceded by scouts. The rate of advance will be guided by the artillery barrage, which lifts 100 yds in 2 minutes. The rear waves should invariably close on the front at each halt. As the objective is reached the rear lines become merged into the front line.

5. At 1.20 the position will be assaulted.

6. Immediately after the assault the captured position will be consolidated, positions for strong points being selected by O.C. W and X Coys. Working parties, if required, will be furnished by Y and Z Coys. O.C. Z Coy. will send up all material carried by his Coy. and both Y and Z Coys. will provide as many shovels and picks as may be required.

7. 2/Lt. Pearson will push up (1) Grenades. (11) S.A.A. (111) Wire (1V) Water.

8. Gas Helmets are to be carried ready for instant use.

9. The Dressing Station will be in 2nd AVENUE, just W of 88th TRENCH. When the Battalion is at BEAUCOURT ROAD the Dressing Station will be in STATION ALLEY.

10. No man is to fall out to attend to the wounded.

11. O.C. Z Coy. will arrange for the disposal of all prisoners.

12. 2/Lt. Rose-Cleland will be in charge of a Bombing Party to move up STATION ALLEY. A Lewis Gun from W and X Coys. together with 2 Stokes Guns will also be under his charge.

13. Men are to be warned that the water they carry with them from ACHEUX may have to last them for 24 hours.

14. All enemy rifles and ammunition should be collected, and used in case our rifles are damaged.

15. Headquarters will be in F STREET when the Battalion assembles prior to leaving our lines. Thence, moving via F STREET and Y RAVINE to

Operation Orders dated 26th June 1916.

- 2 -

STATION ROAD. Communication should be by messenger via STATION ALLEY.

                                                Lieut. & A/Adjt.
                                                1st R.D.F.

Copy No. 1 - 7   Headquarters
          8 - 9   W Coy.
        10-11   X Coy.
        12-13   Y Coy.
        14-15   Z Coy.

APPENDIX A.

1. Places of Assembly:-
   W Coy. in ESSEX STREET, its left on BROADWAY.
   X Coy. in ESSEX STREET, its right on BROADWAY.
   Y Coy. in 88th TRENCH, its left on BROADWAY.
   Z Coy. in 88th TRENCH, its left on 2nd AVENUE.

2. Coys. will move to the front line as under;-
   W and Y via BROADWAY and F STREET.
   X and Z via 2nd AVENUE and BLOOMFIELD.

3. <u>Dress</u>. Marching Order without packs. The haversack, with iron rations, on the back. 120 rounds S.A.A. Officers will dress the same as the men, and will carry rifles. A tin disc will be carried on the outside of the haversack.

4. <u>Tools and Stores</u>. Coys. will draw as below;-

   W Coy;- From Quartermaster.
       20 shovels, 10 picks.
       30 wire cutters.
       15 hedging gloves
       20 wire cutters (rifle)
       4 diamond screens
       15 flares.
       Bombs.

   From Dump.
       30 shovels.
       4 trench ladders.
       5 Bangalore Torpedoes
       300 sandbags.

   X Coy;- 20 shovels, 10 picks.
       30 wire cutters.
       15 hedging gloves
       20 wire cutters (rifle)
       15 flares
       15 flares
       Bombs.

       30 shovels.
       4 trench ladders
       5 Bangalore Torpedoes
       300 Sandbags.
       4 diamond screens

   Y Coy;- 100 shovels, 20 picks.
       15 wire cutters
       10 hedging gloves
       15 flares
       Bombs.

       4 trench ladders.
       4 diamond screens
       300 sandbags.

   Z Coy;- 100 shovels, 20 picks.
       15 wire cutters
       10 hedging gloves
       15 flares
       Bombs

       4 trench ladders
       4 diamond screens
       600 sandbags
       12 wood stakes
       3 hammers
       3 mauls
       10 rolls barbed wire
       10 rolls French wire

5. The advance over the German front system will be on a frontage of 2 Coys. in line of platoons in platoon column at 50 yds. interval and 100 yds distance. Our leading line will be 300 yds. from rear of the Royal Fusiliers. W Coy. will direct, its right marching 50 yds north of Y RAVINE.

6. The Battalion will attack on a frontage of 2 Companies in line of platoons in platoon column, extended to 5 paces, and a distance of 40 yds between lines. W and X will be in front, Y in support 50 yds. behind the leading companies. Z will be in reserve 100 yds behind Y.

7. All Coys. must guard their flanks.

8. Platoon Signal Discs will be carried in the leading sections.

9. All Officers and N.C.Os will carry 4 flares.

SECRET

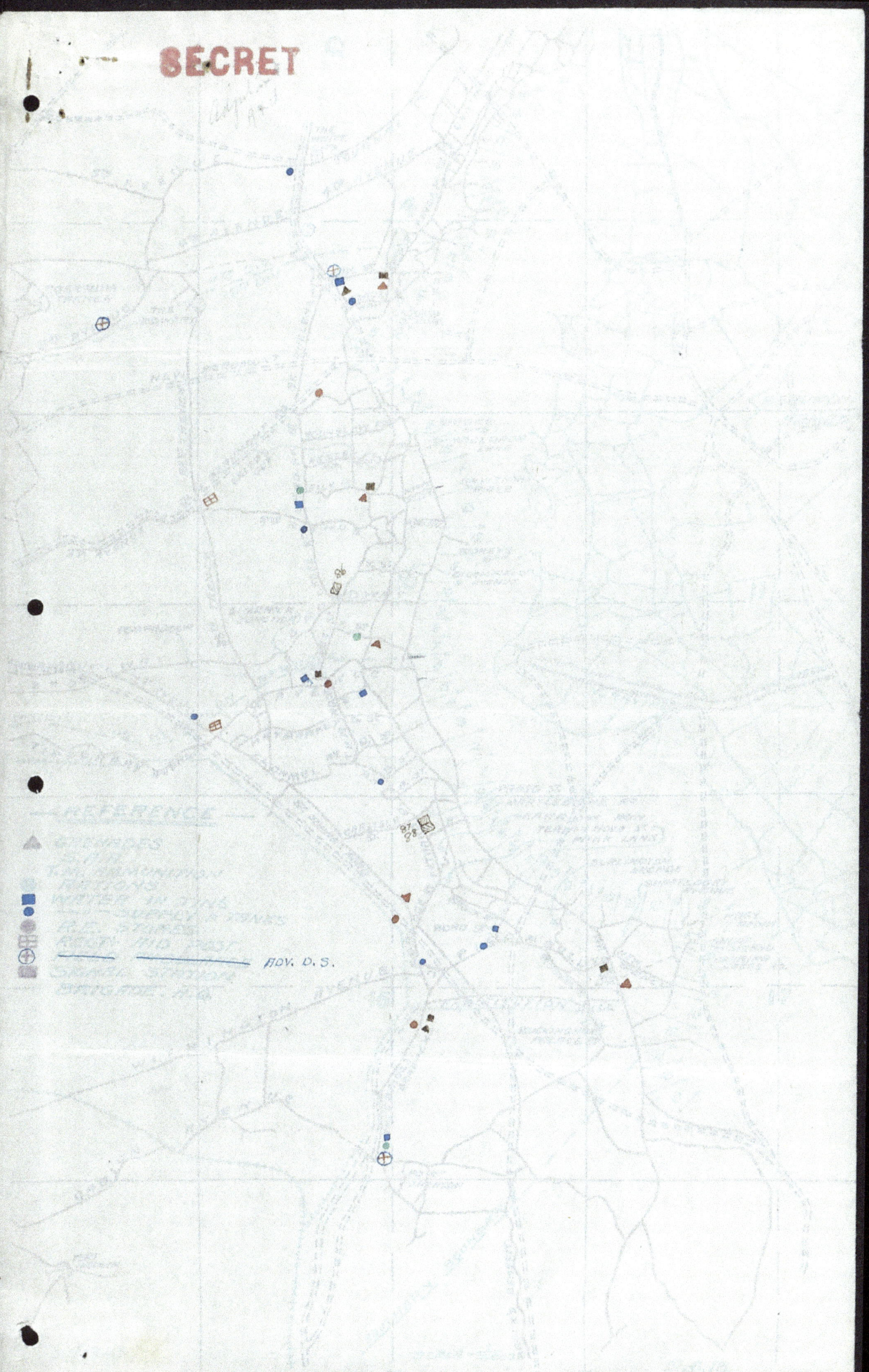

Copy No. 3

G 46

13th June 1916

1. The Northern Area of the Division will be as follows:-
Q 4 D 2.8 to Q 4 C 5.9, thence South of 3rd AVENUE to the road junction Q 2 D 5.2, thence across railway at Q 8 A 9.5, thence a straight line to the MAILLY-ENGLEBELMER road at the road junction Q 13 B 2.2.5.

2. The road by which troops will go up to the trenches will be from ENGLEBELMER to Q 14 A 10.00, then by TIPPERARY and BROADWAY.

Officers, N.C.O's and runners must be made acquainted with this road during the next two days.

for Brig.General, Cmdg. 86th Inf. Brigade.

Copy No. 1	2nd Royal Fusrs.	Copy No. 9	Brigade Major
" " 2	1st Lancs. "	" " 10	Staff Captain
" " 3	1st R.Dublin "	" " 11	Intelligence Officer
" " 4	16th M'sex Regt.	" " 12	87th Brigade.
" " 5	86th Bde. M/ce Gun Coy.		
" " 6	86/1 T.M. Battery		
" " 7	86/2 T.M. "		
" " 8	G.O.C.		

29th Division.
86th Infantry Brigade.

1st BATTALION

ROYAL DUBLIN FUSILIERS

JULY 1 9 1 6

86/29.

War Diary

of

1st Bn Royal Dublin Fusiliers

for

July 1916

Army Form C. 2118.

WAR DIARY
or
INTELLIGENCE SUMMARY.
(Erase heading not required.)

1 R Dublin Fus Vol 4

3.X.
6 sheets

Place	Date	Hour	Summary of Events and Information	Remarks and references to Appendices
Firing Line MAILLY	1/7/16		Fourth of July, 1916. Reached our allotted positions in trenches – from BROADWAY & at 0100. W Coy (on right) & X Coy (on left) in ESSEX ST. with Y Coy (on right) & Z Coy (on left) in 88th TRENCH. Casualties during these 2 hours slightly invited Bombardment became more intense from 0630 to 0720 – at which hour the Attack was launched. The 2/Royal Fusiliers (on right) & 1/Lancashire Fusiliers (on left) advanced against the German 1st Line trenches immediately in front of Rows 3 Coys. – which was supplemented by us – near BEAUMONT HAMEL at 0720. Immediately the 2/R.F. & 1/L.F. advanced we commenced to move up to the Front Line trenches – W Coy with Y Coy in support of F.ST & BROADWAY and X Coy with Z to sup[por]t of BLOOMFIELD & 2nd AVENUE ready to move up against the German Second Line System of Trenches in BEAUCOURT RIDGE – S.E. of BEAUMONT HAMEL. The Bn. was supposed to move Bn. behind the 2/R.F. by Coys. and advance at STATION RD (also by Coys) ready for the assault of the enemy Second Line System, but this could only take effect the 2/R.F. had cleared these Lyster's... the enemy Front Line System – and this the 2/R.F. were unable to accomplish	

WAR DIARY or INTELLIGENCE SUMMARY

Army Form C. 2118.

(Erase heading not required.)

Place	Date	Hour	Summary of Events and Information	Remarks and references to Appendices
FIRING LINE (AUCHONVILLERS)	1/7/16	cont.	It was very difficult for Coy to move up to the Front Line owing to the trenches being blocked by a number of men of the Bn in front (1/R.F.), 86th Field M.G. Coy & Stokes Trench Mortar parties. Consequently it was 0800 before W & X Coys were able to begin moving out over the parapet. But our barbed wire was cut only at intervals of about 40" & by this time the Germans had M.Gs trained on these gaps, the result being that my Companies were very heavy. Only a few of our men ever got through our own lines & still fewer of those succeeded in advancing more than 30" or 60" before being shot down. W Coy & Y Coy both blamed unsuccessfully under fire. Z Coy in support to W & Y Coys both blamed unsuccessfully to establish & consolidate our Front Line — X Coy on right & Z on left. Orgar was later ordered to reinforce H. Stokes Trench Mortars abandoned near the German line (on top of some crater at HAWTHORN REDOUBT). Lieut. W.P. OULTON with 20 men went out and attacked & succeeded in covering 2/Lt H. Greene as there & suffering many casualties. Our total casualties for the day numbered Officers: 4 killed (Capt. E.R.L. NEWSHAM, 2/Lts. R.J.W. PEARSON, C.F. GREENHILLS, 9th Queens, and A.P.M.B. AGER CLELAND 3/R.D.F.), 7 Wounded (Lts. R. ELPHIL 3/R.D.F., 2/Lts. T.W.R. NEILL 9/R.S.F., (Reading) W.J. ROBERTSON, 9 R.N.S. Fusiliers, H.V. SPINNIE, 1/R.D.F., F.L.S. DURWARD 10/Royal Scots, J.E.B. MAUNSELL, (/R.D.F. and M.H. TIGHE (/R.D.F.) and 1 missing (2/Lt D.R. WARNER, 1/R.D.F.). O.R Casualties not yet completed, but estimated 300. Taken off strength 4 officers killed 16 officers wounded, 16 O.Ranks killed, 63 O.R. missing, 1 O.R. died.	1 R D F 1st Royal Fus 38 - 477

Army Form C. 2118.

WAR DIARY
or
INTELLIGENCE SUMMARY.
(Erase heading not required.)

Instructions regarding War Diaries and Intelligence Summaries are contained in F. S. Regs., Part II. and the Staff Manual respectively. Title pages will be prepared in manuscript.

Place	Date	Hour	Summary of Events and Information	Remarks and references to Appendices
FIRING LINE	2/7/16		Holding Front Line from SAP 6 (on right) to HAPPY ALLEY (on left). Carrying forward wounded & dead from Carnoy & clearing	
(AUCHONVILLERS)	3/7/16		clearing & repairing trenches. Casualties Nil	38 - 979
"	4/7/16		Holding Front Line & continuing yesterday's work.	39 - 979
"			Relieved Northumberland Reg.t (A & B Bn. on right) & Royal Irish Fusiliers (1st Division on left). (1st Brigade off.)	38 - 979
MAILLY WOOD	5/7/16		Relief complete by 9.30 p.m. moved by Platoon down to Reserve in MAILLY WOOD	38 - 979
- do -	6/7/16		Bn. resting & cleaning up. Bn supplying 500 men for working parties for various members	
			(Numbers approx.). Staff of 1st OR. arrived (MAJ SCOTT OR March off Strength MD) Casualties Nil	37 - 974 / 37 - 974
			Bn on fatigues working parties & a commencement made at training specialists	37 - 973
- do -	7/7/16		- do -	28 - 972
- do -	8/7/16		- do -	28 - 972
- do -	9/7/16		- do -	Casualties Nil
- do -	10/7/16		- do -	Casualties Off. Nil OR. 2 killed 1 wounded 28 - 769
- do -	11/7/16		- do -	Lt W.E. CHADBECK to H.Q. 28 - 767
- do -	12/7/16		- do -	Lt F.H. McCORMICK promoted. O.R. 2 rejoined 27 - 769
- do -	13/7/16		- do -	Off. Nil O.R. 9 wounded, 10 rejoined 27 - 764
- do -	14/7/16		Orders to relieve 16th Middlesex tomorrow in Front Line - do - 1 " 1st " 27 - 777
- do -	15/7/16		Relieved 16 sex. Reg.t in Front Line - Left of Rifle Section (see Trench Map attached). Trench line further to right than	

Army Form C. 2118.

WAR DIARY
or
INTELLIGENCE SUMMARY.
(Erase heading not required.)

Instructions regarding War Diaries and Intelligence Summaries are contained in F. S. Regs., Part II. and the Staff Manual respectively. Title pages will be prepared in manuscript.

Place	Date	Hour	Summary of Events and Information	Remarks and references to Appendices
FIRING LINE (MESNIL)	15/7/16	(contd)	X Bay (on right) & Z Bay (on left) taking front line — also the potation east of KNIGHTSBRIDGE (Support) Y Bay in Rue at MESNIL. W Bay. Sunken FORTS ANLEY, WITHINGTON, PROWSE, MOULIN. Our previous lines — nearer R. ANCRE. Relief completed by 1700. Draft – 56 OR arrived. Casualties – NIL	27 – 933
	16/7/16		Weather fine. New bn. Trenches very bad — Unknown in all direction. Very large amount of work ahead. Gun to front. Foreign & main communication trenches into state of repair. Our shell attack lasting from 2300 to 0100 — very heavy, but shells fell mostly to right rear of our lines. Casualties NIL Returned – 18 OR	27 – 837
–do–	17/7/16		Weather showery. Work continued. Draft. 1.7 officers. 98 OR arrived. 2/Lt M F HEFFY, A DALTON, J L R GIBBS & J KILLINNEY (Y Bay) and E SHESHY & T H L ADDIS (Z Bay)	3 it – 949
–do–	18/7/16		Weather improving – also trenches. Work going on well – especially X Bay line. Garrison of FORTS ANLEY and WITHINGTON relieved & moved to MESNIL. Casualties – NIL	34 – 9435
–do–	19/7/16		Work going on steadily. Both fairly quiet. Lent considerable amount of shelling at night mainly — especially from S.G.S & T.M's. Officers & joined – Lt H M B GUN-CUNINGHAM (W Bay), A F TELFER (X Bay) C H GRAHAM (Y Bay) and 9 T HERNON (Z Bay) and 12 OR rejoined	38 – 956
–do–	20/7/16		Weather good & work progressing. Orders to prepare for another "push" — on opposition to our front. Line Dyoken N of ANCRE R. Heavy bombardment of our front line at 2305. 2335. Casualties. NIL	36 – 955
–do–	21/7/16		Bombardment commenced last night lasted for about 1½ hrs & was chiefly ground working parties (our own & MONMOUTH PIONEER Bn). Y has across while it lasted. Casualties 1 Off (N/ ADDIS) wounded. 6 OR Killed & 12 OR wounded. Another short bombardment commenced at 2315.	24 – 928

1577 Wt.W10791/1773 500,000 1/15 D. D. & L. A.D.S.S./Forms/C. 2118.

Army Form C. 2118.

WAR DIARY
or
INTELLIGENCE SUMMARY.
(Erase heading not required.)

Instructions regarding War Diaries and Intelligence Summaries are contained in F. S. Regs., Part II. and the Staff Manual respectively. Title pages will be prepared in manuscript.

Place	Date	Hour	Summary of Events and Information	Remarks and references to Appendices
FIRING LINE (MESNIL)	21/7/16	(cont)	Summary of Reinforcements sent to the fire line army post fortnight:- R. Dublin Fus 514, R. Munster Fus. 52, R. Inch. Regiment 63, Leinsters 19, R. Irish Fus. 9, R. Irish Rifles 41, R. Innis killing Fus. 11, Connaught 2.	37, 928
-do-	22/7/16		Patrols reported to Bde. but reply received from Division that there was no enemy. Bombardment commenced last night continued with increased intensity until 0230, in our working parties on Front line and a barrage put on our support lines & communication trenches. The line evidenced back to Coy's in Reserve lines & formed 16 new front line fragments. Heavy howitzer Field Guns Trench mortars & T.M.'s used by enemy. Our retaliation very feeble. Not progressing pretty well. Day quiet — except for our customary intense bombardments at intervals of each lasting for 5-10 minutes — and provoking no response from enemy. I.T.CHLOSECK reported annihilated by CHLOSECK. Casualties — 3 O.R. Killed, 9 O.R. wounded.	
-do-	27/7/16		That night very quiet. Relieved X & Z in Front Line by W & Y. Z & by LE MESNIL. Relieved by 10th CHESHIRES — Relief complete 2000. Bn marched down to WARNIMONT WOOD — arriving at midnight.	36, 9.15
-do-	23/7/16		Orders for relief by 7 Bde. Relieved by 10th CHESHIRES — Relief complete 2000. Bn marched down to WARNIMONT WOOD — arriving at midnight. Casualties — 2 O.R. wounded.	36, 9.11
WARNIMONT WD	24/7/16		Orders to move to BEQUVAL. Move completed 1530. Long morning of men made to complete march.	36, 9.11
BEQUVAL	25/7/16		Morning devoted to interior Economy Afternoon short route march. Bathing parade. (364)	36, 9.11
-do-	26/7/16		Morning Route March. Afternoon — Bathing parade. 7/LT. P. F. HENCHY (W.Coy), B. B. MURPHY & F. DOWLING (Z) 39 — 9.11 joined Bn.	

Army Form 2118.

WAR DIARY
or
INTELLIGENCE SUMMARY.
(Erase heading not required.)

Instructions regarding War Diaries and Intelligence Summaries are contained in F. S. Regs., Part II. and the Staff Manual respectively. Title pages will be prepared in manuscript.

Place	Date	Hour	Summary of Events and Information	Remarks and references to Appendices
BEAUVAL	27/7/16		Orders to entrain at DOULLENS at 2019 for HAZEBROUCK. Left BEAUVAL at 1145 and halted for dinner on road. Passed into DOULLENS at 1800 & entrained. Trains out at 2025.	39 - 911
WORMHOUDT	28/7/16		Detrained at ESQUELBECQ at 0130 & marched out to WORMHOUDT - arriving 0520. Billets very scattered but not the Bn. two got their own bags at disposal J.O.C. Corps for interior economy. Official report received that Lieut. R LAW commanded to ENGLAND Casualties Nil Reported 2 ort.	38 - 913 38 - 3 <s>913</s>
- do -	29/7/16		Training carried on under Coy. arrangements.	
- do -	30/7/16		Rcy'd. inst. Orders to move tomorrow to CAMP J near POPERINGHE	38 - 909
- do -	31/7/16		Reveille 0330. Moved over to CAMP J (Trans from WORMHOUDT to POPERINGHE - nine miles) & arrived in Bn. Durham Light Infy - Trans Camp abt 2p 1330. Bn't Camp Bn. have got moved into.	38 - 901

Walter Capt
2/Lt 1/R Dublin Fus
1/8/15

ORDERS FOR THE MOVE
by
Lieut. Col. H. Nelson, D.S.O.
Commanding 1st Royal Dublin Fusiliers,
Thursday, 14th July, 1916.
Friday In the Field.

The Battalion will move up to the trenches and take over from the 13th Middlesex Regt. tomorrow afternoon, on the left of the Brigade sector, "X" Coy. on the right in the front line, and "Z" on the left in the front line, "W" and "Y" Coys. in support. "W" and "Y" Coys. will take over the dugouts in MESNIL, at present occupied by the Royal Fusiliers.

1. The Battalion will move by platoons in the following order, X, Z, W, Y. The first platoon will leave at 1400, the remainder following at at least 200 yds. distance.

2. O.C. Coys. the R.S.M. and C.S.Ms, the Machine Gun Officer, with *all* the Lewis Gunners ~~from X and Z Coys.~~, the Signalling Officer, with Signallers, and the Regimental Bombing Officer, with the Reg. Bombing Sgt. and Cpl. will proceed to the trenches during the morning, as usual.

3. O.C. Coys. will report in writing to the Adjt. before leaving the huts, that their lines are left clean and in a sanitary condition. They will also report in writing to the Adjutant on the condition of the dugouts and lines taken over by them, and immediately upon the relief of their respective Coys. being completed, will report to the Adjutant by Orderly.

4. O.C. Coys and the Lewis Gun Officer will make arrangements with the Quartermaster for drawing Very Pistols, Periscopes and Wire Cutters.

5. Lieut. Clarke will inspect all huts and lines after the Battalion has moved out, and will report to the Camp Commandant, and, if necessary, accompany him round the lines. He will also render a report in writing to the Adjutant.

6. Lieut. Barry, with two N.C.Os to be detailed by O.C. "X" Coy. will march in rear of the last platoon of "Y" Coy. to collect any stragglers, and bring them in a formed body to Battalion Headquarters.

7. Blankets, in rolls of 10 to be at the Quartermaster's Stores by 0900 tomorrow. Overcoats will be carried in packs.

8. Coy. stores, Officers' Kits and Orderly Room Stores will be packed ready for removal at 1400.

9. The Transport Officer will have one limber per Coy. and one limber for Orderly Room and Headquarter Officers' Kits, as near as possible to the various Headquarters at 1400. The Lewis Gun Officer will arrange with the Transport Officer regarding limbers required. All spare limbers will be at the Quartermaster's Stores at 1400.

10. O.C.Coys. will ensure that their respective Coys. move out completely equipped, special attention being paid to Gas Helmets, Steel Helmets, Iron Rations and Field Dressing, & *Identity Discs.*

Lieut. & A/Adjt.
1st R.D.F.

29th Division.
86th Infantry Brigade.

1st BATTALION

ROYAL DUBLIN FUSILIERS.

AUGUST 1 9 1 6

Vol 5

4 X
9 sheets

CONFIDENTIAL

WAR DIARY

OF

1st Battn ROYAL DUBLIN FUSILIERS

FROM 1st August 1916 To 31st August 1916

Volume XVII

WAR DIARY or INTELLIGENCE SUMMARY

Army Form C. 2118.

Place	Date	Hour	Summary of Events and Information	Remarks and references to Appendices
POPERINGHE (Camp "J")			For month of August 1916.	
	1/8/16		Training & cleaning up Camp. That convenient camp were not been in — but does not seem particularly sanitary. Capt W.T. SCOTT joined Bn & posted to Y Coy.	39 - 901
-do-	2/8/16		Bn Route March — very warm day & exceptionally dusty road. Afternoon cleaning Camp.	39 - 892
			7 Othrks transferred to M.G. Coy (869)	
-do-	3/8/16		Orders to move to Camp "O" situate E of POPERINGHE. Move completed by 2200.	39 - 891
Camp "O"	4/8/16		2/Lt P.J. NOONAN joined Bn & posted to X Coy.	40 - 891
-do-	5/8/16		Training and cleaning up this camp.	40 - 887
			Route March — Bn to Baths during day.	
-do-	6/8/16		Day of Rest. Lieut F.A. WILSON relinquished duties of A/Adjutant (as S.I.S. 15" 5/8/16) & took over Command of Y Coy.	
			Capt H.L. RIDLEY relinquished Command of Y Coy & took over duties of A/Adjutant.	40 - 888
-do-	7.8.16		Training carried on as usual. In the afternoon Brigade Sports were held at Bde H.Q. in which the Battn did well. 2/Lt C.D. Matthews (from the Inniskilling Dragoons) and C.R.T. HEARN (3rd R.D.F.) joined the Battn. and both posted to W Coy.	42 - 887
-do-	8.8.16		Left Camp O at 2045 and marched to the Krain (3 miles away) which took us to YPRES ASYLUM where guides from the 2nd S.W. Borderers met us and conducted us to the dug-outs on the	

WAR DIARY
or
INTELLIGENCE SUMMARY.
(Erase heading not required.)

Army Form C. 2118.

Place	Date	Hour	Summary of Events and Information	Remarks and references to Appendices
CANAL BANK YPRES	9.8.16		on the Canal bank where we were to spend the night in Brigade Reserve. In the meantime the GAS horn had sounded and the guns opened up on our front. It was only a local attack of gas which did not come on our immediate front. Eventually the S.W.B.'s left at 0030. Two platoons of Y Coy were at an advanced post at LA BRIQUE, about a mile nearer the firing line. The dug-outs were excellent, facing the Canal, about ½ mile North of YPRES. A fine sunny day spent in getting ready to move up to-right. We left at 2045 starting with H. Coy and Coy following at 4hr interval. 16th Middlesex took over from us on the Canal bank, and we relieved the 1st Border Regt. in the firing-line. Relief took a long time as the heavy guns were late in arriving; relief complete by 0230. Two Coys X LINE; Y Coy in reserve in ST JEAN right, X on the left; Z Coy in support in the "X LINE"; Y Coy in reserve in ST JEAN were also Battn. H.Q. are situated. We are the left sub-sector of the left sector of the Divisional front. Our front is known as the WIELTJE SALIENT.	4.2.887
FIRING LINE (WIELTJE)	10.8.16		Work begun on the trenches (numbered B 9, 10, 11, 12 on the Trench Map) which were in a very bad state. There was practically no parados, the parapet too low and not bullet-proof, no dug-outs to speak of, and the line littered with old tins and rubbish which had been accumulating for months. The wire in front was very poor. Owing to the state of the trench work was only possible by night.	4.2.887

WAR DIARY
or
INTELLIGENCE SUMMARY.

(Erase heading not required.)

Army Form C. 2118.

Place	Date	Hour	Summary of Events and Information	Remarks and references to Appendices
FIRING LINE	11.8.16		day & night, and during the day it is necessary to avoid as much movement as possible. After dark, work was begun in front of B9 & 10 and work on the front line trenches continued.	42.880
do	12.8.16		Quiet day with the exception of a few shells in B9 and JOHN STREET; two casualties. Work, as last night, continued.	42.878
do	13.8.16		Coys Commander visited trenches in the early morning with the G.O.C. Division. As a result, work was discontinued and all efforts concentrated on putting the trenches more in order, on salving kit and clearing along lines and refuse left in the line. Fairly heavy bombardment of B9 & 10 by Minenwerfers – no casualties. Mule trench a good deal knocked about. Quiet day. A few shells into ST JEAN about 11 p.m., which wounded one transport horse. Two men wounded, one to Hospital. 2/Lt HENCHY and 25 O.R. returned from bombing course.	42.878
do	14.8.16		The Coys. in the front line were relieved at night, W & Y Coy xxx X & Z Coy instead of having the whole of two Coys in front line by day, two platoons each of Y and Z Coys in future will be left in ST JEAN, and from there they will go up each night to work in the front line. Some small shells into B10 in the early morning which knocked the parapet about to some extent. 2/Lt HORROM and 3 N.C.O.'s went to the Div: School. Capt SCOTT takes over charge of the Lewis guns.	42.875
do	15.8.16		Fine and quiet day. Work continues on B9 & 10 and JOHN STREET principally.	42.875

Army Form C. 2118.

WAR DIARY
or
INTELLIGENCE SUMMARY.
(Erase heading not required.)

Instructions regarding War Diaries and Intelligence Summaries are contained in F. S. Regs., Part II. and the Staff Manual respectively. Title pages will be prepared in manuscript.

Place	Date	Hour	Summary of Events and Information	Remarks and references to Appendices
FIRING LINE	16.8.16		Enemy bombarded B9 and 10 with heavy trench mortars off and on for two hours & one artillery retaliation. Three casualties, one killed, rest all wounded. No shell shock. GAS ALERT on about mid-night and at 2.45 a.m. Strombos horns sounded. We stood to with helmets ready but after a little time it turned out to be a false alarm.	42.875
do	17.8.16		No shelling. Work continued at night. Some rain during the day which made the trenches sloppy. 2/Lt Wickham returned from Hospital (never struck off). Ten men in Hospital and thirty-six returning. Ten casualties struck off.	42.862
do	18.8.16		G.O.C. Division round trenches in the early morning – very pleased with the work done during the last week. Some more rain. Quiet day and no shelling.	
do	19.8.16		Trenches muddy with the rain which lasted on and off most of the day and towards evening became fairly heavy. Battn. relieved in the evening by the 2nd S.W. Borderers. Relief completed by mid-night. We took over billets in YPRES from the Hampshire Regt.; getting in by 0130.	42.862
			CAPT TRIGONA embarked for England 16.8.16. One man wounded and 5 struck off.	41.856
CONVENT YPRES	20.8.16		The Battn. is spending its time in billets. H.Q. and X Coy are at the CONVENT (nearest to YPRES). Cloth Hall. Coy H.Q. and 2 Platoons of Y Coy are at VLAMERTINGHE on detachment. The billets in YPRES are in cellars, very dark and damp. There were no parades as it is Sunday.	41.856

Army Form C. 2118.

WAR DIARY
or
INTELLIGENCE SUMMARY.
(Erase heading not required.)

Instructions regarding War Diaries and Intelligence Summaries are contained in F.S. Regs., Part II. and the Staff Manual respectively. Title pages will be prepared in manuscript.

Place	Date	Hour	Summary of Events and Information	Remarks and references to Appendices
CONVENT YPRES	21.8.16		Quiet morning, but at 1500 we bombarded the enemy trenches with heavy shells for two hours. There was some retaliation on YPRES and two shells hit the CONVENT without doing any damage. While here we have permanent working parties amounting to 10ff 86 O.R. daily for work under R.E. & Town Major and a maintenance party on WEST LANE. Remainder of Battn. short 23 O.R. went up to the trenches in the front line in the right Section and worked on trenches S.21 a.2. A.1 and 2. Very muddy and bad trenches in every way. Party left at 2100 and returned 0500.	
"	22.8.16		Gas alarm of GAS at 2030 and another at 2230. 2/Lt ADDIS reported from Base Hospital. Quiet day. While here the General wishes a daily to be forward in the middle of the day. Working parties the same as yesterday. 2/Lt HENCHY admitted to Hospital (not struck off.) 1 man struck off.	42. 856 42. 855
"	23.8.16		Routine and working parties as usual.	T.P.5.14/6 42. 855
"	24.8.16		Same as yesterday. Div wire to say that Capt R. LAW and 2/Lt H.J. ROBERTSON are awarded Military Crosses.	42. 850
"	25.8.16		Working parties as usual at night. A patrol of 4 Germans walked into the trench our party was working on. 2/Lt GIBBS fired six shots at them and they disappeared after throwing a shovel which luckily did not explode. No further trace of the patrol. One man wounded slightly.	
"	26.8.16		Instead of the usual work, all available men were turned onto wiring MUD LANE on to extreme right of the Divnl front. Excellent work done - wire from G.O.C. Div. to congratulate all ranks.	42. 849

WAR DIARY
or
INTELLIGENCE SUMMARY.

(Erase heading not required.)

Army Form C. 2118.

Place	Date	Hour	Summary of Events and Information	Remarks and references to Appendices
CONVENT	27.8.16		Lieut. and Qr. Mr. ARMSTRONG left the Battn. for England to report to the War Office, as the result of his application to be transferred home. He joined the Battn. in EGYPT in January and has served continuously with the Battn. since then, doing most excellent work. Lieut Clarke took over duties of Qr. Mr. Three men struck off from Hospital; one transferred to ENGLAND for employment.	41. 845
YPRES	28.8.16		Sunday - only permanent patients out in the day. At night 200 men on carrying Gas cylinders to front line. No shelling. One O.R. to Hospital.	41. 844
Do	29.8.16		Battn. postponed by one day owing to Gas Operations, 130 O.R. on carrying parties at night, remainder at Camp. No working parties owing to relief. ESSEX REGT were supposed to relieve us but at the last minute, about 2100, it was changed and we were told the 1/8 MIDDLESEX were to relieve us. They had to come down from the front line, and as our train back was due to leave at 2345 we did not wait for them. Our train from YPRES ASYLUM was an hour late owing to a false Gas alarm earlier in the evening. It began raining hard about 1800 and continued for the rest of the evening. Eventually the train arrived and after our mile's march we reached Camp 'O' at 0130, which had been vacated by the ESSEX 3d Hd.	41. 844
CAMP 'O'	30.8.16		A pouring wet day. Camp much the same as when we were here before. More drains dug and nothces (notices) for Officers' Mess and Mess huts for the Coys instituted, and a Sergts mess. All specialists are attached to H.Q. Coy.	41. 841

WAR DIARY
or
INTELLIGENCE SUMMARY.

Army Form C. 2118.

Place	Date	Hour	Summary of Events and Information	Remarks and references to Appendices
			This morning was given up to interior economy and clothes fitting. Batts. went to the baths at POPERINGHE, beginning with "C" Coy. at 1300 and the other Coys at 1 hr intervals. One platoon of Z Coy is on detachment at REIGERSBURG, a post about 3/4 mile West of the Canal. 18 O.R. struck off. 2/Lt KILLINGLEY and 18 O.R. went off to Div. Bombing Course.	41.823
CAMP "O"	31.8.16		Training began; parades:- 6.45–7.45 Physical Training; 9–12.30 Coy. Training; 2–4 Lectures, Musketry etc. All specialists under their own officers. Instructional parade at 5.30 for all Officers and N.C.O's. One man rejoined from Hospital.	41.824

H. L. Ridley Capt.
R. Dub. Fus.
a/Adjt

29th Division.
86th Infantry Brigade.

1st BATTALION

5/6 ROYAL DUBLIN FUSILIERS

SEPTEMBER 1 9 1 6

Vol 6

Confidential   M/L 8B

War Diary

of

1st Bn. Royal Dublin Fusiliers

from 1st September to 30th September
1916

Volume 2~~+~~

Army Form C. 2118.

WAR DIARY
or
INTELLIGENCE SUMMARY.
(Erase heading not required.)

Instructions regarding War Diaries and Intelligence Summaries are contained in F. S. Regs., Part II. and the Staff Manual respectively. Title pages will be prepared in manuscript.

Place	Date	Hour	Summary of Events and Information	Remarks and references to Appendices
			For the Month of SEPTEMBER 1916	EFFECTIVE STRENGTH
CAMP "O"	1.9.16		Training continued as on previous days.	41 823 O.R
do	2.9.16		Battn. route-march in the morning. In the afternoon an hour's drill for officers and N.C.O's. W, X, Y & Z Coys played in Brigade football competition 7.30 beforein the morning. Hostilities resumed	41 823
do	3.9.16		Sunday. No work on parades except for Divine Service. The Coys Commanders visited the Camp in the morning. Weather fine. 2/Lt. Hollom and N.C.O's returned from Div. School. Three O.R in Hosp. Struck off.	41 820
do	4.9.16		Parades as usual. In the afternoon work was begun on a new model trench but rain interfered with progress to some extent. Twelve O.R. in Hospital struck off.	
do	5.9.16		Rain most of the day. Parades could only be held in the huts. War gas schools of the smaller bore respirator types have been issued and Coys are having parades and drill in them with gas instr. of adjustant. 2/Lt TROTTER and MOTTHEWS and 3 Sgts to Div School. Three O.R. rejoined.	41 802
do	6.9.16		Training continued. Practice in contact Patrol in the afternoon for the Bde. 2/Lt. Downing and Special team 2/Lt. Oxley (atta. T.M.B) transferred to General list and struck off. CAPT CARRUTHERS went off on 7 days	41 811
do	7.9.16		Parades as usual. In the evening there was a Brigade Concert.	40 811
do	8.9.16		Battn to Div. Baths in POPERINGHE in the morning. beginning with W Coy. at 0800. Packing up made up to CANAL BANK in the evening. left Camp for the train at 1930 and	40 811

1772

WAR DIARY or INTELLIGENCE SUMMARY

Army Form C. 2118.

Place	Date	Hour	Summary of Events and Information	Remarks and references to Appendices
CANAL BANK	9-9-16		Roch over fire the 2 WSWB by 2230 on the CANAL BANK. Deputations as before — Z Coy sent over flares and a Lewis gun to the 2/o BRAVE post. LIEUT OXLEY struck by a man 19.16.7 D.R. to Hospital	41. 804
YPRES			Day spent preparing to go up to the front line in the evening. Lewis Gunners Bombers reconnoit in the afternoon. Remainder left in the evening beginning with X Coy at 1930 and relieved the 1st Border Regt. in the left subsector of the right sector with H.Q. at ST JEAN. No hitches. Relief complete by 1300. X and W Coys held the night and left of the front line respectively. Y Coy in the X lines and Z in ST JEAN. Some work done after settling down. Capt WILSON & S.M. DOYLE to 2nd Army School. 4 & 2 to the	41. 800
FIRING LINE	10-9-16		Trenches are more muddy than when we were here before, otherwise very little change. Work during the day on X8 and B11+12 j at night some wiring done and repair of B9+10 and 10AR (?). Weather fine. Two O.R. to Hospital.	41. 798
ST JEAN				
Do	11.9.16		Some Minnenwerfers over B9+10 in the early morning when the G.O.C. Division was going round the trenches. Some shells over ST JEAN for several hours in the afternoon. No one wounded. Capt OULTON went to first course at VIII Corps Senior Officers' School. One man wounded.	41. 797
Do	12.9.16		Quiet day. Some rain during the evening. Trench railway continued with the laying of even rails. Work as usual. One man to Hospital	41. 796
Do	13.9.16		Dull day with some rain. Work as usual. 2Lt DOWLING and 8 O.R. returned from Lewis Gun Course	41. 796

1732

Army Form C. 2118.

WAR DIARY
or
INTELLIGENCE SUMMARY.
(Erase heading not required.)

Instructions regarding War Diaries and Intelligence Summaries are contained in F.S. Regs., Part II. and the Staff Manual respectively. Title pages will be prepared in manuscript.

Place	Date	Hour	Summary of Events and Information	Remarks and references to Appendices
FIRING LINE	14.9.16		Very little shelling. Some showers during the day. Relieved by 16th Middlesex Regt. in the evening and took our way into the CANAL BANK vacated by that regiment. Relief complete by 22.30. Deplorable state of camp the same as five days ago. X Coy supplied an Officer and three men for 2ⁿᵈ BRIQUES.	4.7.30
CANAL BANK	15.9.16		Quiet day. Working parties at night took 250 men for work in ADMIRAL'S TRENCH and B.10.A. While here we have 7 men of the Div. Reserve (G) attached to us for rations and accommodation. 2/Lt Voorend admitted to Hospital (not struck off). Pnr. RICKMAN A Y Coy, shot at 0600 for desertion. Draft of 22 N.C.O's and 8 men arrived in the evening. Fair number have been out before and are very useful as we are getting short of N.C.O's	41. 825 41. 814 41. 813
Do.	16.9.16		Working parties as yesterday. 11 O.R. to Hospital	
Do.	17.9.16		Fine day. Although Sunday working parties are required as usual in the evening. Our men were pouring wet all day. At night starting at 19.00 we relieved the Hampshire Regt. in the firing line in the left subsector of the right section. Y & Z Coys in the front line in the right and left co-	
Do.	18.9.16		facturly. W Coy in support in the X lines. X Coy in reserve half in the X lines and half in PoT.II2E. H.Q. at PoT.II2.E. WOOD. Our front extends from A.1 to 5. until the Crater on the right about 100ᵗ away from the GERMAN trenches. Trenches are very wet and muddy of St Chevair. Relief complete by 22.40. From 2 a.m. went off or chewin the early morning — the platoons just 2 O.R. injured	41. 815

174L

Army Form C. 2118.

WAR DIARY
or
INTELLIGENCE SUMMARY.
(Erase heading not required.)

Instructions regarding War Diaries and Intelligence Summaries are contained in F. S. Regs., Part II. and the Staff Manual respectively. Title pages will be prepared in manuscript.

Place	Date	Hour	Summary of Events and Information	Remarks and references to Appendices
FIRING LINE	19.9.16		Fine day. The trenches and left very dirty, muddy and full of refuse and two Work begun on cleaning up and draining trenches. Nothing. Drafts of 7 N.C.O's and 8 men joined up in the evening.	41.930
POTIJZE	20.9.16		Rain most of the day. Trenches very wet and falling in. As the result of an attempted raid on the early morning by the Royal Fusiliers on our immediate left the enemy retaliated with artillery and 2/Lt OXLEY and 2/Lt GRAHAM, attached 86th T.M.B., were killed being buried in the trench where they were to fire from, along with their team. Difficult to do much work in the rain, and drainage was the chief occupation. Wire from Capt HAWES (29th Div. School) saying he was going as Staff Captain to the 103rd Brigade 2/Lt HEENAN attached 86th T.M.B. to Hospital (not struck off).	39.930
Do	21.9.16		Enemy shelled our front in the early morning. Wounded one man. Work continued as usual. Draining and rebuilding trenches. 4 O.R. Off on leave. 8 O.R. to Hospital.	39.822
Do	22.9.16		Quiet and fine day. Work as usual. Two O.R. wounded.	39.820
Do	23.9.16		Corps Commander and Kinsella in the early morning. Fine sunny day. Returns in the evening of the Middlesex Regt. Relief complete 21.45. We took over billets in YPRES vacated by that regiment, with H.Q. at the CONVENT and Coys in the same billets as when we were here a month ago. No detachment at VLAMERTINGHE but 1 officer and 25 men for W. Coy at HUSSAR FARM. New POTIJZE 2 O.R. wounded. Two men in trans.	39.818

175/2

Army Form C. 2118.

WAR DIARY
or
INTELLIGENCE SUMMARY.
(Erase heading not required.)

Instructions regarding War Diaries and Intelligence Summaries are contained in F. S. Regs., Part II. and the Staff Manual respectively. Title pages will be prepared in manuscript.

Place	Date	Hour	Summary of Events and Information	Remarks and references to Appendices
CONVENT	24.9.16		Sunday. Fine sunny day. After divine service Coy fitted new clothes and boots. 110 men on working parties	
YPRES.			by day and 100 by night, chiefly under R.E. supervision. Capt COLLINS evacuated to ENGLAND, with	
			rheumatism (old attack of old wound) 2 men wounded.	3.9. 8.20
Do	25.9.16		Quiet day. Working parties as normal. 6 O.R. to Hospital stuck off Coy ground	38. 8.15
Do	26.9.16		No shelling. Work as yesterday	38. 8.15
Do	27.9.16		Coys Commander round our billets in the morning. Work as usual. Three men gone leave.	3.9. 8.15
Do	28.9.16		Day working parties as usual. In the evening the Battn moved down to Camp C. having moved	
			by train at 22.30 The Middlesex Regt took over the CONVENT and we relieved the Hampshire Regt	
			in Camp C. All settled in camp by midnight. 2/Lt. TROTTER and MATTHEWS and 3 Sergts	38. 8.12
			rejoined from Div. M. School. Three O.R. to Hospital.	
CAMP "C"	29.9.16		Battn to baths at POPERINGHE during the day, starting with M.G.s, 1st N.C.Os.. In the evening we moved	
			into Camp "O" and took over from the Essex Regt. Relief completed by 12.30. Inspections in camp	
			as they were a few weeks ago. One man off on leave. Lewis Gun course HAMIE and 2/Lt P13.53 and 2 Sergts to Div. School	38. 8.12
CAMP "O"	30.9.16		Paraded 6.45 – 7.45 Physical Training. 9.15 – 10.15 Company Drill (as many as possible) 10.15 – 12.15 Training	
Do			of Specialists and Coys continued. 1/Lt HOLCOM and 8 O.R. to ETAPLES on leave from Cross 2 O.R. to Hospital.	38. 8.10
			At about 16.30 the Battn were suddenly called upon to provide a working party of 10 offrs and 400 O.Rs. by cable handed that night	

H.L. Ridley Capt
1. R. Dub. Fus
a/Adj

1.10.16

29th Division
86th Infantry Brigade.

1st BATTALION

ROYAL DUBLIN FUSILIERS

OCTOBER 1 9 1 6

Vol #7

6 X sheets

Confidential

17M

War Diary
of
1st Battn Royal Dublin Fusiliers

From 1st October 1916   To   31st October 1916

Volume 22

Army Form C. 2118.

WAR DIARY
or
INTELLIGENCE SUMMARY.
(Erase heading not required.)

Instructions regarding War Diaries and Intelligence Summaries are contained in F. S. Regs., Part II. and the Staff Manual respectively. Title pages will be prepared in manuscript.

Summary of Events and Information

For the Month of OCTOBER 1916.

Place	Date	Hour	Summary of Events and Information	Remarks and references to Appendices
CAMP "O"	1.10.16		Sunday – no parades. Coys Commanders thought the Camp in the morning. Two men in Hospital with Influenza.	Effective Strength Officers 38, O.R. 826
(NR POPERINGHE)	2.10.16		Heavy rain most of the day. Short parade in the morning owing to expected move tomorrow.	38 . 826
do	3.10.16		Move postponed for 24 hrs. Parade in the morning. In the afternoon Coys Commanders inspected and addressed their Battn. on our leaving is Camp ('B'). One man to Hos. struck off. Draft of 2 O.R. joined.	38 . 827
do	4.10.16		Wet all morning. Doing the loading of the Transport which left by road for WORMHOUDT with Cookers & Gun Carts at 0930. The Battn left "O" Camp at 1300 for POPERINGHE where we entrained on the light railway and eventually left at about 1650. After 2 hrs wait we reached WORMHOUDT at 1845 and proceeded to the same billets as those occupied by the Battn two months ago. The transport had already arrived and everyone was settled in by 2000. LIEUT GEN CUNINGHAME and 2/Lt C.1235 attached in the morning from the Div School.	38 . 827
WORMHOUDT	5.10.16		Parades :- 9.15 – 12.15 , 2 – 4 Company and Specialist Training	38 . 827
"	6.10.16		Parades as yesterday with the addition of 7 – 7.30 Physical Training. 3 O.R. in Hospital of S.D.R. rejoined from the Battn. parade at 9.15 for ceremonial. Exhibition of Guard Mounting by C.S.M. HARVEY'S class of 12 Senior Infants who have been instructing for the last ten days. This is the first Regimental class of its kind to be sent on an ex-	38 . 829
"	7.10.16		-cellent. Afternoon and evening – preparing to move South. Tanglecliff Heads to POPERINGHE at midnight. Bn O.R. Struck off. Parade at 0300 and proceeded to WORMHOUDT Station, which we left by train at GWS for POPERINGHE – 2 kilometres Battn and Transport entrained again at HOPOUTRE Siding, near POPERINGHE and left at 1000 for LONGPRE on AMIENS	38 . 826

WAR DIARY
or
INTELLIGENCE SUMMARY.
(Erase heading not required.)

Army Form C. 2118.

Instructions regarding War Diaries and Intelligence Summaries are contained in F. S. Regs, Part II. and the Staff Manual respectively. Title pages will be prepared in manuscript.

Place	Date	Hour	Summary of Events and Information	Remarks and references to Appendices
LA NEUVILLE (nr CORBIE)	9.10.16		All day spent in the town LONGUEAU was reached at 23.45	37.926
			Battn left LONGUEAU at 0130 for billets at LA NEUVILLE (about nine miles away) which was eventually reached at 0645. Marching was clear as blankets were carried on the men - also the guide lost his way. Billets not very good - chiefly barns - and not very sanitary. 2/Lt Hallon and 8 O.R. reported for duty from Canadians. Capt Kinnear and C.S.M. Davis for 2 Army School. LIEUT CAMERON and 2 N.C.O's left at 1900 as billeting party	
do	10.10.16		Battn paraded at 0900 with Transport and marched to DERNANCOURT (about 10 miles away) which was reached by 1415. Billets poor - barns for the men & 15 officers in house new-sides in tents. Draft of 44 O.R. posted interviewing. 2/Lt HEENAN (attd. T.M.B.) invalided to ENGLAND	38.926
DERNANCOURT	11.10.16		No parades, only inspections. Some officers went to see the line in the morning	37.870
do	12.10.16		No parade in the morning & Some Coys bathed in the river ANCRE. In the afternoon the Battn marched and practised the attack. One O.R. went on leave. H.o.R. in Hos. struck off	37.873
do	13.10.16		Battn paraded at 0800 and marched to a camp by the S.E. corner of MAMETZ WOOD which was reached by 11 a.m. The camp consists of French shelters in trenches and a few bng-ots. The rest of the day was spent in settling down. 3 O.R. in Hos. struck off	37.869
MAMETZ WOOD	14.10.16		Parades 7-7.30 Physical Training 9-12 Coy and Specialist Training. The camping ground is full of salvage of every description, a great quantity of which has been collected	37.866

Army Form C. 2118.

WAR DIARY
or
INTELLIGENCE SUMMARY.
(Erase heading not required.)

Instructions regarding War Diaries and Intelligence Summaries are contained in F. S. Regs., Part II. and the Staff Manual respectively. Title pages will be prepared in manuscript.

Place	Date	Hour	Summary of Events and Information	Remarks and references to Appendices
MAMETZ WOOD	15.10.16		Sunday. Divine Service at 10 a.m. Afterwards shot attack practised by Coys. Cleaning camp continued. One O.R. on leave. Draft of 14 O.R. joined 14.10.16	37.880
Do	16.10.16		Parade 9.15 – 12.15 by Coys. During bombing practice by X Coy. in the course of the morning a Mills-type grenade exploded in the middle of a party and injured Capt CARRUTHERS M.C. Lt BARRY 2/Lt TROTTER and 12 OR all of whom were taken off to F. Hos. The exact cause of the accident is uncertain but was due to the rifle grenade not leaving the muzzle of the rifle after being fired. 7/Lt SAFERY left for England on special leave. 9 O.R. went to Base H.Q. as Pioneers for Divn.	
				34.853
			2.O.R. transferred to R.E. 11 O.R. on Mn Khuleeff	34.847
Do	17.10.16		The Battn. went to the baths at VIVIER MILLE (6 miles away) During afternoon and evening. Col & Wet Sgts Band sister left.	34.847
Do	18.10.16		Expecting to move up into the line we went most of the day. Heavy rain nearly all day. At 1030 orders were received that two Coys. (X + Z) were to take over and	
Do	19.10.16		for the trenches. Remainder of the Battn. left at 14.30 and marched to the trenches N.W. of GUIDECOURT. Roads in very muddy and bad condition. Dispositions in the line are :— X + Z Coys. take over from 10th Regt. in SMOKE TRENCH ; W and Y Coys. in front line relieved the Berkshires. Regt. H.Q. in Dug-outs on BULLS ROAD just N.E. of FLERS. Relay not complete till 0100. Owing to the appalling condition of the roads and trenches Transport going to Property REDOUBT (on trenches confuse the left subsector of the left sector of the Divn Area.) Draft of 17 OR joined yesterday.	180h 34.864

T2134. Wt. W708–776. 500000. 4/15. Sir J.C. & S.

Army Form C. 2118.

WAR DIARY
or
INTELLIGENCE SUMMARY.
(Erase heading not required.)

Instructions regarding War Diaries and Intelligence Summaries are contained in F.S. Regs., Part II. and the Staff Manual respectively. Title pages will be prepared in manuscript.

Place	Date	Hour	Summary of Events and Information	Remarks and references to Appendices
FIRING LINE FLERS	20.10.16		The guns are all very wet and cold as in places the trenches are up to the knees in and among the slush many men became shell fast in the mud. The trenches are few and shallow and very muddy; the ground all round being covered with shell holes. Difficult to send rations and water up to the front line and it can only be done at night. During the day there was intermittent shelling round H.Q. and the support lines (SMOKE TRENCH). Relief can reach H.Q. – and all rations and water come up on pack mule. The only cog. possible in what we do or have done in the front line even tho' is not always possible. The R.S.M. (BAKER) was wounded in the morning and Q.M.S. MELIS takes over R.S.M. 2 O.R. wounded	34 962
do.	21.10.16		Frost in the early morning & fine and sunny rest of the day. Trenches drying up well but still very muddy. Work was begun on making a new Assembly Trench in front of the line in Nomansland. At night 1 and 2 Coys. relieved W and Y. in the front line on the right and left respectively. 2/Lt. HENCHY wounded than 2 O.R. killed and 16 O.R. wounded.	33 847
do.	22.10.16		We continued at night on the new trench in front. Fine day - not much shelling. 2/Lt. HEGRVIS Smitted to Hos. (not struck off) 2/Lt. DOWLING to Hos. with shell shock. 3 O.R. killed; 7 O.R. wounded.	32 834
do.	23.10.16		Relieved at night by 2nd Royal Fusiliers and on relief (complete by 0/20) the Battn. marched to Bpe. to DELVILLE WOOD and took over lines vacated by that regiment. The country was very wet and heavy, and the men wet and weary. Some Coys. were delayed by those preceding in the	1812

T2134. Wt. W708-776. 500000. 4/16. Sir J. C. & S.

Army Form C. 2118.

WAR DIARY
or
INTELLIGENCE SUMMARY.
(Erase heading not required.)

Instructions regarding War Diaries and Intelligence Summaries are contained in F.S. Regs., Part II. and the Staff Manual respectively. Title pages will be prepared in manuscript.

Place	Date	Hour	Summary of Events and Information	Remarks and references to Appendices
			front line with the result that the two Coys did not reach their firing line till 0630. CAPT W R OUTON M.C. reported from the VIII Corps Officers' School. 2/Lt NOONAN fell out on the way down from the trenches and went to Hos. 10.R. killed. 3 O.R. wounded. 10.R. with a shrivel off.	32.829
DELVILLE WD	24.10.16		Rain most of the day. Lines very bad with only a few dug-outs, mostly shelters made of oil-sheets and a waterproof. The men are played out from want of sleep and hot food during the past 6 days. Carrying parties amounting to 6 offrs and 300 O.R. were required by Bde. at night to follow stores to the forward Bde. dumps. The men were not fit for this work with the result that many fell out & failed at work till 01.00 at 03.00. Casualties from yesterday. 8 O.R.	32.821
do	25.10.16		Nil in morning. Battn. less Y Coy. left DELVILLE WOOD at 16.00 and proceeded to front line trenches where we relieved the Roy. Ens. in the same subsector on the Bayonet Spur except that the Australian Div. on our left had taken over some of the front line. W Coy. in front line. Z and X in SMOKE TRENCH. H.Q. on top. Relief complete 23.15. One O.R. on leave. 10.R. killed 8 O.R. wounded/missing	32.811
FIRING LINE FLERS	26.10.16		Fine warm morning. Trenches drying up. and still very muddy. Draft of 37 O.R. joined Bn. Work at night continued on the Assembly trench in front of 30 m y FT 7 9c night Z, G, relieved W in the front line. 2/Lt HEALY admitted to Hos. 4 O.R. wounded.	32.807
do	27.10.16		Battn. relieved in the evening by 2nd Hampshire Regt. and on relief moved to DELVILLE W.D.	

Army Form C. 2118.

WAR DIARY
or
INTELLIGENCE SUMMARY.
(Erase heading not required.)

Instructions regarding War Diaries and Intelligence Summaries are contained in F. S. Regs., Part II. and the Staff Manual respectively. Title pages will be prepared in manuscript.

Place	Date	Hour	Summary of Events and Information	Remarks and references to Appendices
DELVILLE WOOD	28/10/16		with the same shellfire as before. 5 O.R. wounded. (Draft of 37 O.R. joined yesterday taken in strength)	32.939
			Fine day. Cleaning up after the trenches. LIEUT C. HANDLER (3rd R.D.F.) and 2/LT GRADWELL (1st R.D.F.) joined. 1 O.R. killed. 2 O.R. wounded. 1 O.R. missing. 1 O.R. died of wounds.	34.834
Do	29/10/16		Received orders early that the 4th Australian Battn were relieving us. Advance party left at 0800 for MAMETZ WOOD. [Relief by Australians completed by 1300] and on relief Coys marched independently to MAMETZ WOOD where we took over the same camps as before. Wet day and roads very heavy. 7 O.R. wounded (from yesterday).	34.827
MAMETZ WOOD	30/10/16		Received orders early to move to VILLE-sous-CORBIE. Battn left at 1030 and marched to VILLE which was reached in the pouring rain by 1530. Billets in barns and houses quite good. Rain most of the day.	34.827
VILLE-sous-Co 31/10/16 -RBIE			Left VILLE at 1130 and marched to CORBIE (dist 6½ miles) which was reached by 1430. Battn billeted in stables and barns — quite good. 1 horseman billets. LIEUT TWEEDY (3rd R.D.F.) and 2/LT KIDSON (5th R.D.F.) joined. 1 O.R. previously reported missing — now in Field Ambulance.	36.828

H. d. Ridey Capt
a/adj 1st R. Dub. Fus.

1831
MB

1.11.16

29th Division
86th Infantry Brigade.

1st BATTALION

ROYAL DUBLIN FUSILIERS

NOVEMBER 1 9 1 6

Confidential

War Diary

of

1st Battn. Royal Dublin Fusiliers

From 1st to 30th November 1916

Volume 23

Army Form C. 2118.

WAR DIARY
or
INTELLIGENCE SUMMARY.
(Erase heading not required.)

Instructions regarding War Diaries and Intelligence Summaries are contained in F.S. Regs, Part II. and the Staff Manual respectively. Title pages will be prepared in manuscript.

Place	Date	Hour	Summary of Events and Information	Remarks and references to Appendices
				Effective Strength
				Offrs / OR's
CORBIE	1.11.16		For the month of NOVEMBER 1916. No parades. Cleaning up after the trenches. All Coys. bathed during the afternoon and evening. Capt OULTON and C.O. went on leave.	36 / 826
Do	2.11.16		Wet morning. Baths. was inspected in the afternoon by H.R.H. The DUKE OF CONNAUGHT. 2/LT GIBB on leave. 7 O.R. rejoined.	36 / 833
Do	3.11.16		Parade 9-1. ; Coy. and Specialist training. First day. One O.R. on leave. 18 O.R. in Hospital. Offr. Died. Injured	36 / 817
Do	4.11.16		" " Shooting on the range by X & Z Coys. 8 O.R. rejoined for 40	36 / 825
Do	5.11.16		Sunday. Church parade in the morning.	36 / 825
Do	6.11.16		Parade 9-1. Shooting on the range by W & Y Coys. 1 O.R. on leave.	36 / 825
Do	7.11.16		Wet morning. Baths made as ordered, were cancelled; instead inspection in billets. 3 O.R. known injured	36 / 822
Do	8.11.16		Parade 9-1. Shooting on the range by Lewis Gunners. 1 man on leave. 2/Lt HEARNE invalided & Eng. sent 20.10.16. 28 O.R. in Hos. struck off.	35 / 794
Do	9.11.16		Parade 9-1. Coy. and Specialist training. 1 O.R. 5 Ho.	35 / 793
Do	10.11.16		Attack practice in the morning on the downs outside the town in front of the Bigadier	35 / 793
Do	11.11.16		Parade 9-1. Rejoined from Ho. 10 O.R.	35 / 903
Do	12.11.16		Sunday. Church parade in the morning. Capt A.B. BAGLEY (1st RDF) joined with a draft of 10 O.R. and posted to command X Coy. 1 man on leave. 2/Lt MATHEWS taken over command of W Coy. from Capt MCFEE on	

1852

WAR DIARY or INTELLIGENCE SUMMARY

Army Form C. 2118.

Place	Date	Hour	Summary of Events and Information	Remarks and references to Appendices
			Capt Scott from commanding X Coy. This was dutie of times from officers from 2/Lt Horton & aug. 2/Lt P.J.	
			Noonan invalided to ENGLAND 30.10.16. Draft of 9 o.r. joined 11.11.16 taken on 3 O.R. & H.Q.	35·819
CORBIE	13.11.16		Parade 9-1. Short Battⁿ. parade in the afternoon Lieut Chandler accidentally injured during landing practice	34·819
do	14.11.16		Inspection by G.O.C. Division in the morning. Afternoon Battⁿ. took part in an assault scheme before him 2/Lt Blair White (9th RDF) joined and posted to X Coy. Capt Hawes. Staff Capt⁶	
			103ʳᵈ Bde. struck off. 13 o.r. to H.Q. Lieut Col Cunningham & 2/Lt Gibbs returned to do schools.	34·806
do	15.11.16		Parade 9.1. 2/Lt Green (atta. 86th F.M.B.) struck off. 1 o.r. & H.Q.	33·805
do	16.11.16		Left Corbie at 11.30 and marched to Meaulte which was reached by 14.30. Billets in former quarters ind. Frosty fine day. 5 O.R. & H.Q. Draft of 6 O.R. joined 15.11.16. 2/Lt Kickham & 10 o.r. attached(?)	33·806
MEAULTE	17.11.16		Clean party day. No parades. 2/Lt Healy yesterday went to Albert to supervise arrival / draft to the Datt.	33·806
do	18.11.16		Left Meaulte at 10.40 and marched to Carnoy Camp (Suzika) which was reached by 14.00. Battⁿ. accommodated in Nissen huts — very good. Some snow in the early morning which turned to heavy rain later in the day. 7 O.R. to H.Q. 14 O.R. sent to Base, permanently unfit.	33·785
CARNOY CAMP	19.11.16		Sunday. No parades. Had we not in Div¹ Reserve. 2/Lt Sheehy (returning from leave) reported as Sigₒ. Offⁱ. / 1ˢᵗ Anzac Corps	32·785
do	20.11.16		Attack practices in the morning. Work round camp in the afternoon. 7 o.r. on leave.	33·785
do	21.11.16		The Battⁿ. moved from Carnoy to Bernafoy Camp in the afternoon, where	1162

Army Form C. 2118.

WAR DIARY
or
INTELLIGENCE SUMMARY.
(Erase heading not required.)

Instructions regarding War Diaries and Intelligence Summaries are contained in F. S. Regs., Part II. and the Staff Manual respectively. Title pages will be prepared in manuscript.

Place	Date	Hour	Summary of Events and Information	Remarks and references to Appendices
			and relieved the 1st ESSEX REGT by 16.15. The Battn is in shelters and dug-outs with the Officers in tents. Two hundred O.R. on working parties. 2/Lt F. MOONEY (late Sergt in 1st Irish Guards) joined and posted to X Coy. 9 O.R. in Hospl. struck off.	34. 776
BERNAFAY CAMP	22.11.16		The whole Battn., about 300 strong, engaged on working parties by day and night, chiefly for the Tunnelling Coy. Fine frosty day. 10.O.R. on leave.	34. 776
Do	23.11.16		Some working parties as yesterday. 10.O.R. on leave.	33. 776
Do	24.11.16		Battn. moved up into the front line in front of LES BOEUFS, starting at 14.30 from Camp. Relief of ESSEX REGT complete by 20.00 – very quick. W and Y Coys. are in the right and left respectively of the front-line in FALL and AUTUMN TRENCHES, together with one platoon of X Coy. Remainder of X Coy in WINTER TRENCH in support. Z Coy & H.Q. Coy in reserve in COW TRENCH. Trenches not very mud as the weather has been fine. 10.O.R. on leave.	34. 776
FIRING LINE (LES BOEUFS)	25.11.16		Rain all day. Trenches in a very bad state and falling in. Three German deserters surrendered soon after dark and were sent down to the Corps Cage. 10.O.R. on leave. Draft of 8 O.R. joined 24th.	34. 784
Do	26.11.16		Fine morning. Men rather exhausted with the mud and want of hot food, the recovering Trenches more than a foot deep in mud in places. Not much work possible, all available men used in carrying rations. 1 O.R. killed and 1 wounded yesterday.	34. 792

T2134. Wt. W708—776. 500000. 4/15. Sir J. C. & S.

Army Form C. 2118.

WAR DIARY
or
INTELLIGENCE SUMMARY.
(Erase heading not required.)

Place	Date	Hour	Summary of Events and Information	Remarks and references to Appendices
FIRING LINE	27.11.16		Frost last night and a fine morning. Relieved at night by the 4th WORCESTERSHIRE REGT. Relief took a very long time owing to mud and the heavy condition of the ground – complete by 0210. Battn marched to CARNOY CAMP. to come into a bytes. 1 O.R. killed and 1 wounded yesterday. 1 O.R. on leave.	34.780
CARNOY CAMP	28.11.16		No parades. Men recovering from the trenches and drying clothes. A fair number of sick but only two really in a bad condition. Fine cold day. 1 O.R. on leave.	34.780
do	29.11.16		No parades. Two hundred and fifty O.R. on working parties. Clothes inspection during day. 2/Lt DALTON went to Corps Railway Employm. Capt Scott on leave (special). 30 O.R. in Hospl. struck off. 21 O.R. sent to Base as unfit on 24.11.16. 1 O.R. on leave.	34.754
do	30.11.16		All available men on working parties. Men recovering gradually after the trenches tho' still a large number reporting sick with sore feet. 27 O.R's in Hospl. struck off. 1 O.R. on leave.	34.727

1882

H. d. Risley Capt
a/adj. 1. RDF.

30.11.16

29th Division.

86th Infantry Brigade.

1st BATTALION

ROYAL DUBLIN FUSILIERS

DECEMBER 1 9 1 6

CONFIDENTIAL. Vol 9

War Diary
of
1st. ROYAL DUBLIN FUSILIERS
from 1.12.16 to 31.12.16.
(Volume 27).

1916

8 x sheets

Army Form C. 2118.

WAR DIARY
or
INTELLIGENCE SUMMARY.
(Erase heading not required.)

Instructions regarding War Diaries and Intelligence Summaries are contained in F. S. Regs., Part II. and the Staff Manual respectively. Title pages will be prepared in manuscript.

Summary of Events and Information

For the Month of December 1916

Place	Date	Hour	Summary of Events and Information	Remarks and references to Appendices
				Effectives Off / O.R.
CARNOY	1.12.16		Moved to BERNAFAY CAMP and relieved the Worcestershire Regt. by 12.45. 22.45 O.R. on working parties during day and night. 2/Lt HOLLOM and 3 N.C.O.'s proceeded to ETAPLES on leave (in Course 3) Wounded (27/11/16)	34 · 724
BERNAFAY CAMP	2.12.16	13.0	O.R. on working parties. Hard frost last night.	34 · 724
do	3.12.16		Relieved Essex Regt. in front line trenches in the evening, leaving BERNAFAY at 14.30. Marching was easy owing to the frost. Relief complete by 20.35. Since last time the line held by the Battn has shifted to the right to the extent of 1 Coy. front. X and Z Coys. on right and left of front line; Y Coy. in support in WINTER and FROSTY TRENCHES; W Coy. in reserve in COY. TRENCH. Dispofn of Bn printed on p.204	34 · 730
FIRING LINE LES BOEUFS	4.12.16		Fine sunny day and trenches not too muddy. Work began on joining up Platoons of X Coy, as there are gaps of 200x and got in them Coy. line. Rations, fuel etc came up by train on the tramway which has just been started. 7 O.R. on leave.	34 · 730
do	5.12.16		Dull morning with a thaw. Work continued. 1 O.R. wounded. 1 man joined 5.12.16	34 · 730
do	6.12.16		Fine day. Relieved at night by Worcestershire Regt and on relief (completed by 19.15) marched to BERNAFAY for the night. All Coys. in camp by 22.30; very quick relief. Good train without any sick or wounded. 2 O.R. wounded	34 · 724
BERNAFAY CAMP	7.12.16		Moved to CARNOY starting at 10.00 and took over same camp as before from Essex Regt.	34 · 722

1901

Army Form C. 2118.

WAR DIARY or INTELLIGENCE SUMMARY.
(Erase heading not required.)

Instructions regarding War Diaries and Intelligence Summaries are contained in F. S. Regs., Part II. and the Staff Manual respectively. Title pages will be prepared in manuscript.

1916

Place	Date	Hour	Summary of Events and Information	Remarks and references to Appendices
CARNOY CAMP	8.12.16		190 O.R. on working parties - chiefly on making a strong point at T 3 Central, which took most of the night. LIEUT GEN CUNINGHAME and 2/LT GIBBS reported from Divl. School. 3 O.R. to 2 O.R. reported	34.727
do	9.12.16		Wet most of the day. No working parties.	34.727
do	10.12.16		Dull day. No working parties. C.S.M. A.R. HOLMAN granted commission as 2/LIEUT and posted to 2 Coy.	35.726
do	11.12.16		Move to MEAULTE leaving at 0900, and reached billets by 1130. Div. is relieved by 20th Div. Major W.P. CLARKE joined and assumed duties of 2 in command vice Major E.F.E. SEYMOUR who is transferred to 2. Bn. (R.D.F) and left this evening. 2/LTs KINNEEN and O'CARROLL joined and posted to W and Y Coy. 4 3 O.R. in Hospl. struck off.	37.683
MEAULTE	12.12.16		Rain most of the day. Advance party left for the next area. 1 O.R. joined.	37.684
do	13.12.16		Left MEAULTE at 1415 and entrained at EDGEHILL at 1600. Arrived LONG PRÉ Known at 2030 and billeted for the night at CONDE (½ mile from station) 2/LT C.V. WICKHAM invalided to ENGLAND. 1 O.R. joined.	36.685
CONDE	14.12.16		Left CONDE at 0900 and marched to SAISSEVAL (about 12 miles away) at which was reached at 1430. Batn. billetted in houses and barns round the village - not very good billets.	36.685
SAISSEVAL	15.12.16		No parades. Cleaning up and inspections. 5 O.R. on leave.	36.685

Army Form C. 2118.

WAR DIARY
or
INTELLIGENCE SUMMARY.
(Erase heading not required.)

Instructions regarding War Diaries and Intelligence Summaries are contained in F. S. Regs., Part II. and the Staff Manual respectively. Title pages will be prepared in manuscript.

Place	Date	Hour	Summary of Events and Information	Remarks and references to Appendices
SAISSEVAL	16.12.16		No parade. 2/Lt KNEAFSEY joined and posted to X Coy.	37 - 685
"	17.12.16		-do- Day of Rest.	37 - 685
"	18.12.16		Training. Parades 0715-0730; 0900-1230; 1445-1600.	37 - 686
"	19.12.16		-do-	37 - 686
"	20.12.16		Battalion Route March.	37 - 681
"	21.12.16		Training. Parades as for 18/12/16.	37 - 681
"	22.12.16		-do-	37 - 681
"	23.12.16		Battalion Route March.	37 - 680
"	24.12.16		No parade. Day of Rest.	37 - 680
"	25.12.16		-do- Xmas Day.	37 - 680
"	26.12.16		Battalion Route March - Draft of 8 O.R. joined unit.	37 - 668
"	27.12.16		Training. Parades 0715-0730; 0900-1230; 1430-1600.	37 - 668
"	28.12.16		-do- also Bathing parade.	37 - 669
"	29.12.16		-do- 2/Lt E.H. ROBERTSON joined and posted to Y Coy.	38 - 682
"	30.12.16		Battalion Route March. 9/Lt T.W.H. MASON joined & posted to W Coy. also Draft of 52 O.R.	39 - 734
"	31.12.16		No parade. Day of Rest.	39 - 731

Confidential

War Diary

of

1st Battn. Royal Dublin Fusiliers

From   1st January 1917
To   31st January 1917

Volume 23

Army Form C. 2118.

WAR DIARY
or
INTELLIGENCE SUMMARY.
(Erase heading not required.)

Instructions regarding War Diaries and Intelligence Summaries are contained in F. S. Regs., Part II. and the Staff Manual respectively. Title pages will be prepared in manuscript.

For the Month of January — 1917.

Place	Date	Hour	Summary of Events and Information	Remarks and references to Appendices
SAISSEVAL	1.1.17		New Year's Day - holiday. Brigade Cross Country Run held in the afternoon. 2/Lt MATHEWS joined 31/12/16 and posted to X Coy. 10 O.R. joined and 5 transferred to M.G.C.	W. Stringth Officer Comdg O.K. 38. 727
do	2.1.17		Training continued. 2/Lt A.L. KENT joined and posted to Y Coy.	39. 727
do	3.1.17		" " Assault practice before the Brigadier. Capt BAGLEY to FLEXICOURT Army School.	39. 727
do	4.1.17		2/Lt HERNON took over temporary command of X Coy. Training continued. Capt F.A. WILSON left the Battn to proceed to ALDERSHOT there to attend the 2° Senior Officers' Course. He has served 17 months continuously with the Battn. Draft of 20 O.R. joined.	39. 747
do	5.1.17		Training continued. 6 O.R. to base unfit. 1 to England as servant to Capt Wilson, who is also struck off.	38. 740
do	6.1.17		G.O.C. Division's inspection and attack scheme. 2/Lt McINTYRE joined from Scots Guards - posted to Z Coy.	39. 740
do	7.1.17		Sunday. Armourer Sgt joined.	39. 741
do	8.1.17		Training continued. Lieuts CONSIDINE and BONNOR joined and posted to Z and Y Coy.	41. 741
do	9.1.17		Left SAISSEVAL at 10 a.m. and marched to QUESNOY (9 miles) where we billetted for the night. 2 O.R. to No A1.	41. 739
QUESNOY	10.1.17		Left QUESNOY at 6 a.m. and marched to AIRAINES where we entrained and proceeded to CORBIE, which was reached at 11.30 a.m. Battn in same billets as two months ago. 2/Lt GREEN joined the Battn for the 88th T.M.B., with two Stokes guns, posted to H Coy, and assumes duties of Battn. Bombing officer.	42. 739
CORBIE	11.1.17		Left CORBIE at 10.30 a.m. and marched to MEAULTE where we billetted for the night. Attn (2.30 + 42. 739	42. 739

Army Form C. 2118.

WAR DIARY
or
INTELLIGENCE SUMMARY.
(Erase heading not required.)

Instructions regarding War Diaries and Intelligence Summaries are contained in F. S. Regs., Part II. and the Staff Manual respectively. Title pages will be prepared in manuscript.

Place	Date	Hour	Summary of Events and Information	Remarks and references to Appendices
MEAULTE	12.1.17		Left MEAULTE at 10.30 a.m. and marched to CARNOY CAMP no 6 where Battn was settled	42. 739
		2 p.m.	Under orders of 17th Div., until our Div. takes over on 16th Jan.	42. 741
CARNOY	13.1.17	14.30	Left CARNOY at 14.30 and marched to GUILLEMONT camp, which we reached 16.30	
GUILLEMONT	14.1.17	15.15	Left GUILLEMONT at 15.15 and proceeded to front line, where we relieved the 9th W. RIDING R. in the left subsector of the Div. line. H.Q. East of MORVAL. J, W, Y & Z Coys in front line with one platoon each of X Coy attached to Y & Z Coys. Remainder of X Coy in reserve at Battn. H.Q. Relief complete 19.40. Way up to trenches is good with duckboards all the way. 21 officers come up to the line – remainder left at CARNOY, where the details and Q.M. Store remain. Draft of 2 O.R. joined.	42. 743
TRENCHES RVAL SECTOR	15.1.17		Quiet day with little shelling. Work carried on at night of forming up places in front line. Movement by day impossible, and only method of communication with front line is over the open.	42. 743
do	16.1.17		Relieved at night by 16th Middlesex Regt. Relief complete by 20.30. Battn returned to CARNOY – all in good. Roads frosty and 'going' good. No casualties this tour.	42. 743
CARNOY	17.1.17		No parades. Fall of snow last night. Draft of 6 O.R. joined.	42. 749
do	18.1.17		do	42. 749
do	19.1.17		Battn. attended Dressing Station in the morning for new trench feet treatment. Left CARNOY	

Army Form C. 2118.

WAR DIARY
or
INTELLIGENCE SUMMARY.
(Erase heading not required.)

Instructions regarding War Diaries and Intelligence Summaries are contained in F.S. Regs., Part II. and the Staff Manual respectively. Title pages will be prepared in manuscript.

Place	Date	Hour	Summary of Events and Information	Remarks and references to Appendices
			at 1430 and marched to GUILLEMONT, same camp as before, which was reached 1615. 12 O.R. evacuated; 1 transferred to M.G.C.	42.736
GUILLEMONT	20.1.17		Relieved 4th Worcestershire Regt. in same sector of trenches as before. Relief complete 1930. Work begun passing up posts in front line; some were put out on the left. Ground is still covered with snow which shows parties up very much at night.	42.736
FIRING LINE	21.1.17		After stables at H.Q. in the morning, and 1 dugout blown in. Fair amount of shelling during the day, more than last time. Work continued at night. Draft of 21 O.R. arrived 1900.17	42.757
do	22.1.17		Relieved at night by 16th Middlesex Regt. - relief complete 1930. Battn. all back in CARNOY camp by midnight. 1 O.R. killed.	42.756
CARNOY	23.1.17		No parades. 2/Lts DUNNE and MAGUIRE joined 1915.17 adjutants to Z and W Coys. 3 O.R. wounded 21.1.17 and 22.1.17. 1 O.R. died in CARNOY camp. Draft of 23 O.R. joined 1915.17	44.775
do	24.1.17		Short parade and running exercise in morning. Snow and hard frost still continuing. 1 O.R. accidentally shot himself with revolver. 1 Sgt. proceeded to cadet school STOMER. 3 O.R. evacuated.	44.770
do	25.1.17		Left CARNOY at 1500 and marched to GUILLEMONT for the night. 2/Lt P.B. BURROUGHS joined on parade to Y Coy. 10 O.R. evacuated.	45.769
GUILLEMONT	26.1.17		Left GUILLEMONT at 1345 and relieved 4th Worcesters in the front line. Relief	

Army Form C. 2118.

WAR DIARY
or
INTELLIGENCE SUMMARY.
(Erase heading not required.)

Instructions regarding War Diaries and Intelligence Summaries are contained in F. S. Regs., Part II. and the Staff Manual respectively. Title pages will be prepared in manuscript.

Place	Date	Hour	Summary of Events and Information	Remarks and references to Appendices
FIRING LINE MORVAL SECTOR	27.1.17		complete by 2010. Y, X, and Z Coys are on the right, centre and left of the front trench. 1 platoon of W in attacks 6 x 5. Remainder of W Coy and details up to 50 in number on left at GUILLEMONT for carrying purposes. 2/Lt O'SULLIVAN finds and patrols to Y Coy.	45.769
			Owing to operations on our immediate left by the 27th Bde which proved successful, the day and night were lively, with abundance of shelling, but not many casualties were caused by it. Little work was possible owing to the same cause. Snow still on the ground and nights very cold. Lieut T.J. CONSIDINE (attd 86th Bde Mining Co) and 1 O.R. wounded.	44.768
do	28.1.17		Relieved at night by 16th Middlesex. Relief complete by 2030. All the Battn in camp at CARNOY by 0030. 1 O.R. wounded.	44.767
CARNOY	29.1.17		No parades. Still cold with snow on the ground. 2/Lt O'SULLIVAN (joined 28.1.17) taken on I.O.R. killed.	45.766
do	30.1.17		Short parade and running exercise in the morning. 5 O.R. wounded (on 27th) 1 to 28th) struck off. 1 O.R. rejoined from desertion. 1 Sgt to Engrs for cadet school.	45.761
do	31.1.17		Trench foot treatment in the morning. Moved to GUILLEMONT for the night starting at 15.30.	45.761

H.L. Ridley Capt
Comdg 1. R. Dub. Fus.

31.1.17

Confidential

86/29

10 X
17 sheets

Vol II

War Diary
of the
1st Bn. Royal Dublin Fusiliers

From   1st February 1917
To   28th February 1917

Volume 26.

Army Form C. 2118.

WAR DIARY
or
INTELLIGENCE SUMMARY.
(Erase heading not required.)

Instructions regarding War Diaries and Intelligence Summaries are contained in F. S. Regs., Part II. and the Staff Manual respectively. Title pages will be prepared in manuscript.

For Month of FEBRUARY 1917

Place	Date	Hour	Summary of Events and Information	Remarks and references to Appendices
GUILLEMONT	1/2/17		Relieved 1st Worcesters in line. Relief complete by 20.05. Some dispositions to before.	45 S.Q. O.R. 761
FIRING LINE NORTH SECTOR	2/2/17		Quiet day. Work at night chiefly carrying up materials as ordered by 16th Bde HQ.	45 761
DO	3/2/17		Relieved at night by 16th Middlesex Regt. Relief complete by 20.45. Battn. came by train from GUILLEMONT to CARNOY. All in camp by midnight.	45 761
CARNOY	4/2/17		Hut occupied by C.O., 2i/c in command, and adjutant destroyed by fire in the morning. Some documents of regimental interest also burnt. No parades. Lt-Col H. NELSON D.S.O. admitted to Hospital; Major N. P. CLARKE takes over command.	45 761
do	5/2/17		Battn. employed on working parties during the day. 10.R. wounded during not (on) 60.R. evacuated	45 754
do	6/2/17		Left CARNOY at 11.00 and marched to MEAULTE (which was reached by 13.00) and on Battn. billeted for the night.	45 754
MEAULTE	7/2/17		Left MEAULTE at 16.00 and marched to LANEUVILLE which was reached by 14.00. Battn. met billetis in very good billets	45 754
LANEUVILLE	8/2/17		No parades.	45 754
do	9/2/17		Parades for training 9-12.30 and 2-3.30. 26.R. rejoined from H.Q. C.S.M. WADE granted commission in R.D.F. and posted to 8th Bn. 1 Sgt. presented to LONDON and sent to Base for commission.	45 754
	10/2/17		Parade 9-12.30.	45 754

T2134. Wt. W70s—776. 500000. 4/15. Sir J. C. & S.

WAR DIARY
or
INTELLIGENCE SUMMARY.
(Erase heading not required.)

Army Form C. 2118.

Place	Date	Hour	Summary of Events and Information	Remarks and references to Appendices
LANEUVILLE	11.2.17		Sunday. No parades. Lt-Col H NELSON D.S.O. discharged from Hos. and granted leave to the United Kingdom	45 — 754
do	12.2.17		Parade for training 9—12.30, 2—3.30. Draft of 12 O.R. (joined 11.2.17)	45 — 768
do	13.2.17		Paraded as yesterday. 1 O.R. transferred to R.F.C. 4 O.R. to Base. 1 O.R. (AC PLATEAU) Wounded	45 — 761
do	14.2.17		Assault practice at 5.30 a.m. Battn. to CORBIE Baths during. 9 O.R. evacuated	45 — 53
do	15.2.17		Assault practice at 9.30 A.M. Lieuts H L Rudly & Brimfield to Hospital. Lieut R.O. Gilmour on leave	45 — 753
do	16.2.17		Assault practice at 9.30 a.m. Brigadier present. 1 O.R. died from Gun Poisoning. 6 O.R.	45 — 740
do	17.2.17		invalided to England. 16 R granted Commission. 5 O.R. to base hospital. Battalion forming contest at 2 P.M.	45 — 740
do	17.2.17		Mass & Assault practice at 10 A.M. before G.O.C. 2 Lieut (C.B Dex?) joined.	46 — 740
do	18.2.17		Battalion marched from LA NEUVILLE at 10.00 for MEAULTE Huts which were reached at 15.00. 2 O.R.'s base permanently unfit	45 — 738
MEAULTE	19.2.17		Left MEAULTE at 9.30 for MALTZ HORN Camp which was reached by 12.13/14.15	46 — 738
MALTZ HORN	20.2.17		Left MALTZ HORN at 13.00 for Support trenches Batt'n at COMBLES	46 — 738
BOULEAU WOOD	21.2.17		Battalion formed up at HAIE Wood at 18.00 & moved from there to FIRING LINE. Relieved 9.S.10.15 Relief complete 23.20. 1 O.R. ret/unrd from hospital.	46 — 738

Army Form C. 2118.

WAR DIARY
or
INTELLIGENCE SUMMARY.
(Erase heading not required.)

Instructions regarding War Diaries and Intelligence Summaries are contained in F. S. Regs., Part II. and the Staff Manual respectively. Title pages will be prepared in manuscript.

Place	Date	Hour	Summary of Events and Information	Remarks and references to Appendices
FRONT LINE	24/9/17		Quiet day. Right of right company rifle grenaded & bombing out about 30 nm Trench	
FRONT LINE	25/9/17		about 11 p.m. Quite heavy shelling ceased. Relay completed 00.30 hrs Marched to Hardecourt Camp	
HARDE CT CAMP	25/9/17		HARDECOURT Camp at 14.00 for BRONFAY Camp in lieu. Was reached at 18.00	
BRONFAY CAMP	25.9.27		Bn Baths in Corbie. Draft of 40 OR arrived Parade at 14.30. Issued pamphlets re further ground. Draft 5 OR RE Left BRONFAY 5 PM for HARDECOURT Camp which was reached by 16.00 AM.	
BRONFAY CAMP				
HARDECOURT	26/9/27		Left HARDECOURT at 15.00. Had tea on COMBLES. Stood to would to [?] & [?] the A46. 4.6.727 Trench to rear Relief [?] in B in Front Line. Relief Complete by 00.15.	
FRONT LINE	28/9/27		Attacked POTSDAM TRENCH and PALZ TRENCH East of SAILLY-SAILLISEL 45T-T1N3 assembled and held of found objectives taken and held. See Appendix A.	

[signature]

Army Form C. 2118.

WAR DIARY
or
INTELLIGENCE SUMMARY.
(Erase heading not required.)

Summary of Events and Information

Appendix A

Report on operations 28th February/1st March 1917

On the night of 27/28 February 1917, the troops under my command lined up in the trenches on their attack frontage, according to programme. Previous to zero all men got out of their trenches and lay on the forward parapet. On our Artillery barrage falling all went forward.

The numbers taking part in the attack are shown on the attached appendix.

The line moved forward to the tape detailed and on "No man's land". It struck this tape at an angle and pushing on into our barrage did not correct its alignment. The whole line from the Royal Fusiliers to the Lancashire Fusiliers appear to have moved rather too much to its left, and struck its objective rather to the left of where they should have been. The reason for this cannot be definitely ascertained. The barrage on the left are reported to have been rather short but on the right is reported to have been excellent. The barrage lifted and the first objective POTSDAM TRENCH was taken and occupied by Moppers up of the 16th Middlesex Regt. A few Germans in it made no fight with hands up lifted to surrender.

The line advanced again following the barrage and arrived opposite the 2nd objective. The going on the left was sufficiently good to enable the line to keep up with the barrage and disposition of the line kept down owing to the trend. For some minutes however our barrage did not lift off it. One officer stated it did not lift till about Zero+30. The Lt. Stokes Guns also appear to have kept their barrage on their objective too long. The barrage at length lifted and the line sprang forward into PALZ-TRENCH through gaps in the enemy wire EAST and WEST of the junction of WEIMAR and PALZ trenches.

Many casualties had by now been caused by:—

WAR DIARY or INTELLIGENCE SUMMARY.

(Erase heading not required.)

Army Form C. 2118.

(3)

Summary of Events and Information

(1) Our own barrage.
(2) Hostile machine guns from front on left front.

As the men on the left had not come up, Nor. an PALZ TRENCH headed by W. LT. TWEEDY and LT. MCFEELEY turned up it to their left. The enemy were encountered and a fierce fight was carried on with bombs, revolvers and rifles. The Lewis guns were clogged with mud and at first could not be used. LT. TWEEDY was here killed an accounting for some of the enemy and showing conspicuous coolness. After bombing the enemy back about 15 yards no further progress could be made. The position was maintained by forcing down the trench until the Lewis Guns were cleaned and bombs had been collected. Less accounted by LT. GUN CUNNINGHAME who throughout the operations handled his company with great skill & gallantry, LT. MCFEELEY attacked again and bombed the enemy back about another 50 yards. The trench bottom was now impassable for attack, being 18" deep in mud. Enemy snipers also commenced it from a sap running

WAR DIARY
or
INTELLIGENCE SUMMARY.
(Erase heading not required.)

Army Form C. 2118.

Place	Date	Hour	Summary of Events and Information	Remarks and references to Appendices
			to the enemy's rear and casualties were heavy. A block was accordingly made. The middle WEIMAR TRENCH was found to be unoccupied, full of water and blocked. The left Company attacking PALZ TRENCH, suffered from heavy going and were unable to keep up with the barrage, which got right ahead of them. CAPTAIN BAGLEY (in command) appears to have neared PALZ TRENCH on the right of his men and in front of them. He jumped down into it and shot one of the enemy. He saw no more, but noticed that his men were off to his left standing quite outside the enemy line. He shouted to them, but could not be heard. They could see no officers, and Capt BAGLEY reports they thought they had overshot their objective, and they hastily had already crossed two trenches (there are certain double broken trenches short of the first objective.) Capt BAGLEY left PALZ TRENCH and made a move to them and took them towards the PALZ TRENCH but now was more to the left than he had been. By this time hostile machine gun fire was causing casualties, and an	

reaching the enemy wire they were heavily bombed from the trench. They could not force their way through the wire which was reported to have been about 10' thick and nearly intact. Their supply of bombs was exhausted. The enemy bombing and machine gun fire increased and they were obliged to go back to POTSDAM TRENCH the Capt BAGLEY tried to get more bombs, but could not find any. Three of his Lewis Guns had been lost and the team's belt mounded. The carrying parties supporting him had suffered heavily and had dumped their material outside PALZ TRENCH. The Lancashire Fusiliers Attachment had been unable to reach PALZ TRENCH up their communication trench (from POTSDAM to PALZ) and a further advance with this communication trench on his left and unsupported with bombs and without wire in front of him, was deemed unadvisable. He had already lost all his officers and could only find about 12 men of his Company and about the same number of the carrying parties and some of the 3rd Wave all others. Officers were casualties.

WAR DIARY
or
INTELLIGENCE SUMMARY.
(Erase heading not required.)

Army Form C. 2118.

(6)

to to make a strong point where he was being assisted by all the
Troopers up he could find.
The Lancashire Fusiliers appear to have also moved rather more to their
left than was intended, and on reaching POTSDAM TRENCH a mixed
body of Lancashire Fusiliers and Royal Dublin Fusiliers entered the
right Communication trench (i.e. the right of the Lancashire Fusiliers)
and started bombing up it. still held up by the enemy who ran down
it. They then maintained their position occupying their left
objective and eventually both trenches.
The earlier reports from the front were conflicting, and it was
believed that the left Company of the Royal Dublin Fusiliers had
attained their objective but in too narrow a front to link up
with the Right Company. As however reports had been received that
Capt. BAGLEY (left Company R.D.F.) was in touch with the Lancashire
Fusiliers on his left, I believed that all objectives had been gained
with the exception of a gap between BAGLEY and 2/Lt CUNINGHAME

(i.e. Left and Right Coys R.D.F.) The moppers up were therefore left to consolidate this line. Later information however showed that Capt BAGLEY was not with the 2nd Objective Instructions had been given to the carrying wave to return to Battalion H.Q. for material and stores. This however proved impossible owing to sniping and machine gun fire. 2/Lt. McKENZIE therefore went out to ascertain the exact situation and from his report it appeared that the strong point occupied by Capt. BAGLEY was a vital factor, to prevent the enemy from cutting in between the Royal Dublin Fusiliers Coy in PALZ TRENCH and the Lancashire Fusiliers in POTSDAM TRENCH. Capt. BAGLEY reported he could not spare anyone to return to "carry". The moppers up were then consolidating the communication trench leading to the Right Company R.D.F. in PALZ TRENCH and the Royal Fusiliers. 2/Lt McKENZIE report was received at 9.30 A.M. At 11.20 P.M. after a conversation with the Brigade Major, the moppers up were sent up to PALZ TRENCH

Army Form C. 2118.

WAR DIARY
or
INTELLIGENCE SUMMARY.
(Erase heading not required.)

Place	Date	Hour	Summary of Events and Information	Remarks and references to Appendices

To Major CUNINGHAME.

The situation was then as follows and remained so until we were relieved 36 hours later except for alteration in line held by the Royal Fusiliers.

[Sketch map showing PALZ, WEIMAR, WATER, R. FUS., POTSDAM TR. (WATER), TM, ORIGINAL LINE]

The trench mortars on my original front line were detailed at 7.45 A.M. to cover my left flank in PALZ. The T.M. sent forward reached its position in POTSDAM but the gun & crew were knocked out by hostile

Army Form C. 2118.

WAR DIARY
or
INTELLIGENCE SUMMARY.
(Erase heading not required.)

Place	Date	Hour	Summary of Events and Information	Remarks and references to Appendices
			gun fire.
Communication with the Lancashire Fusiliers was extremely difficult owing to water and enemy.
At 2.55 p.m. a German bombing attack on the Right forced the Royal Fusiliers to retire down the communication trench at the junction of Royal Dublin Fusiliers and Royal Fusiliers in DALZ TRENCH. Instructions were telephoned to 2/Lt CUNNINGHAME to assist the Royal Fusiliers in every possible way by supplying material bombs, rifle grenades, Lewis Guns etc. This was done and when the enemy had almost reached my W.Coy. dug out entrances were broken down by 2/Lt. CUNNINGHAME to block the kind and one of his Lewis Gunners used his gun against the attackers. At 2.55 P.M. the attack was held up. The effect of the attack was to expose both my flanks in DALZ Tr. except for the Royal Fusilier blocking party. Both 2/Lt CUNNINGHAME and McFEELEY reported that they feared they could not withstand a	

Army Form C. 2118.

WAR DIARY
or
INTELLIGENCE SUMMARY.
(Erase heading not required.)

night attack and considered a withdrawal necessary. They were told to hang on at all costs, every available man was sent forward with stores, a protective barrage called for, additional Lewis Guns were sent forward from Battalion H.Q. and S.O.S. rockets & bombs asked for. It was at this period that I asked for reinforcements as the C.O. Royal Fusiliers said he had only 125 men left.

At 7.0 pm there was an intense German bombardment and S.O.S. signals went up. Our barrage came down. Enemy were reported moving on my left front but no attack was made. Bombardments continued at intervals until we were relieved.

On March 18t at about noon two German Aeroplanes flew over our lines and signalled to their own troops. The enemy guns then appeared to register on:—

(1) My front line DALZ
(2) POTSDAM
(3) New night communication trench.

WAR DIARY
or
INTELLIGENCE SUMMARY.
(Erase heading not required.)

Army Form C. 2118.

Place	Date	Hour	Summary of Events and Information	Remarks and references to Appendices
			(4) Battalion H.Q. and trench in rear	
			(5) Original British Line	
			(6) Some post in rear of Battalion H.Q.	
			After about 2 hours the aeroplanes flew off. No British machines went up at the time.	
			The following points appear to be worth mentioning:-	
			(1) Men were so anxious to keep close to our own barrage during the advance that they did not stake out into their waves.	
			(2) Some mopping up went to the final objective, others were prevented from doing so with difficulty.	
			(3) Germans declined to surrender in dug outs even when bombed in one case, a Lewis gun was brought up and fired down at they came up.	
			(4) It was a late dawn and no doubt the men could not recognize their officers, throwers greatly felt.	
			(5) About 30 rounds per man S.A.A. were fired, 170 were on the man.	

(6) For trench warfare 50 rounds S.A.A. per rifle and enough sand carried in bombs is suggested.

(7) Bombing attacks are very sudden. Bombs in Coy. Store or dumps cannot be got out in time. Boxes might be built on the parapet or dug into them.

Signed. L. P. Evans Maj.
Commanding 1st Royal Welsh Fusiliers

Confidential

War Diary
of
1st Royal Dublin Fusiliers

From 1st March 1917
To 31st — —

Volume No 27

WAR DIARY or INTELLIGENCE SUMMARY

Army Form C. 2118.

for Month of MARCH 1917

Place	Date	Hour	Summary of Events and Information	Remarks and references to Appendices
1917				
FRONT LINE	1.3.17		Shelled heavily all day. Relieved by NEWFOUNDLANDERS. Relief complete at 0210 on 2.3.17	A.6.727
HARDECOURT	2.3.17		Rear of Battalion reached HARDECOURT at 5.30 P.M. Moved to BRONFAY CAMP at 2.30 P.M. Arrived at BRONFAY at 4.30 P.M.	A.6.727
BRONFAY	2.3.17		Left BRONFAY at 2 P.M. for PLATEAU STATION. Battalion entrained there for BUIRE. Arrived at BUIRE at 5.30 P.M. and Battalion marched from there to VILLE SUR CORBIE. Billets for Battn Ruled HQ & Coy 6 O.R. at Chateau & B Coy 1 Offr & 94 O.R. at 9= O.R. Billets. D Coy 1 Offr & 98 O.R. Billeted 3 Officers & C Coy 1 Offr 19 O.R. Billeted in usual billets at 2nd C.L.R. All inspection had to be postponed owing to weather being unfavourable. Casualties 28.2.17 and 1.3.17 X	
VILLE SUR CORBIE	4.3.17		LIEUT H.L. RIDLEY rejoined from Base and took over duties of Acting Adjutant from 2/LT I.D. MACKENZIE. CAPT. F.S. LANIGAN-O'KEEFFE joined and took over command of X Coy. 2/LT E.A. BYRNE and A.H. ALLEN joined and posted to X and Z Coys.	43.594
do	5.3.17		No parades. Reorganization of Coys. under the new system of making the Platoon a self-contained fighting unit. 2/LT T.J. REILLY joined and posted to W Coy.	[1.3.17, 10.7. & H.Q.] 44.594
do	6.3.17		Coy parades in the morning. CAPT. C.O. MATTHEWS & LT W.B. CAMERON invalided. 2/LT. CAPT A.B. BAGLEY invalided.	41.593
do	7.3.17		Inspection of Battn by Corps Commander at 1000. Afterwards he addressed the Battn. X LT C.M. TWEEDY, 2/LT H. GREEN, F. MOONEY & G.F. GRADWELL. 2/LT W.T. O'CARROLL, J.G.D.B. DUNNS and P.B. BURROUGHS Killed (W. 16.3.2). 2/LT A.L. KENT	

WAR DIARY
or
INTELLIGENCE SUMMARY.
(Erase heading not required.)

Army Form C. 2118.

Instructions regarding War Diaries and Intelligence Summaries are contained in F.S. Regs., Part II. and the Staff Manual respectively. Title pages will be prepared in manuscript.

Place	Date	Hour	Summary of Events and Information	Remarks and references to Appendices
VILLE			and congratulated and thanked it for the success of the recent operations. He also said good-bye on the Division's being about to leave his (XIV) Corps	
	8.3.17		Coy. parades for training 9-1. Lectures and extra instruction in the afternoon.	41. 593
do	9.3.17		do	41. 593
do	10.3.17		do	41. 593
do	11.3.17		Sunday. Divine Service in the morning. Inspection of Platoons by C.O. at mid-day. Owing to weak state of the Coys., Platoons have been reduced to 2 per Coy. Draft of 12 O.R. joins 10.3.17. 21 O.R. evacuated to Hosp.	41. 593
do	12.3.17		Coy. parades for platoon training 9-1. Lectures and extra instruction in the afternoon. LIEUT J.N. BARRY joins and posted to X Coy.	41. 584
do	13.3.17		Coy. parades for Platoon training 9-1. Lectures and extra instruction in the afternoon. Draft of 14 O.R. joins. 4 O.R. to Hospital	42. 584
do	14.3.17		Coy. parades for Platoon training 9-1. and in the afternoon. CAPT W.T. SCOTT invalided to ENGLAND. 8 O.R. to Base, unfit. 5 O.R. to Hospital.	42. 584
do	15.3.17		Coy. parades for Platoon training 9-1 and in the afternoon. See note.	41. 571
do	16.3.17		do	41. 571

15.3.17 CAPT A.B. BAGLEY, LT H.M.B. GUN CUNINGHAME and C.M. McFEELY awarded Military Cross for 28.2.17 Lt. Col. H. NELSON D.S.O.

Army Form C. 2118.

WAR DIARY
or
INTELLIGENCE SUMMARY.
(Erase heading not required.)

Instructions regarding War Diaries and Intelligence Summaries are contained in F.S. Regs, Part II. and the Staff Manual respectively. Title pages will be prepared in manuscript.

Place	Date	Hour	Summary of Events and Information	Remarks and references to Appendices
			returns from leave and takes over command from MAJOR N.P. CLARKE. 13 O.R. under age, attached to 4th Army Inf. School and Prisoners of War Cage, struck off strength. 2/Lt J.L.A. GIBBS detailed for special duty with 4th Field Survey Co. and 1 O.R. struck off. 10 O.R. to Hos. 2 O.R. evacuated to Base.	40.554
VILLE	17.3.17		St Patrick's Day. Platoon training 9–10. Battn. parade for Mass in the village church at 10.30. Remainder of morning and afternoon football matches between Coys. Draft of 10 O.R. joined 16.3.17. 5 O.R. to base, unfit. 2 O.R. rejoined from Hos. 1 O.R. to Hos.	40.560
to	18.3.17		Sunday. Divine Service in the morning.	40.560
to	19.3.17		Coy parades for training 9–1 and in the afternoon. Regtl. Transport left by road for new training area.	40.560
to	20.3.17		Left VILLE at 0830, entrained at EDGEHILL and left at 1000 for AIRAINES which was reached at 1430. Battn. marched from there to MERICOURT EN VIMEUX (5 miles) and were settled in billets by 1700. Draft of 31 O.R. joined 19.3.17. 1 O.R. to Hos.	40.590
MERICOURT	21.3.17		" " Coy. paraded in the morning on the new training ground.	40.590
do	22.3.17		" " Moved to BELLOY ST LEONARD (3 miles) in the afternoon. Better billets than in last village. Draft	

Army Form C. 2118.

WAR DIARY
or
INTELLIGENCE SUMMARY.
(Erase heading not required.)

Instructions regarding War Diaries and Intelligence Summaries are contained in F. S. Regs., Part II. and the Staff Manual respectively. Title pages will be prepared in manuscript.

Place	Date	Hour	Summary of Events and Information	Remarks and references to Appendices
BELLOY	22.3.17		2/Lt A.H. MATTHEWS invalided to ENGLAND (9.3.17) of 21 O.R. joined 21.3.17	39 611
	23.3.17		Coy parades for training 9-1. 10.R. rejoined from Hos.	39 612
	24.3.17		Battn. attack practice 9-12 in training area. Draft of 13 O.R. joined 23.3.17. 10.R. to Base. 9 O.R. to Hos. 1 to Hos. evacuated	39 615
Do	25.3.17		Sunday. Draft of 10 O.R. joined 24.3.17. 10.R. to Base. 2 O.R. to Hos. 1 O.R. struck off as deserter	39 621
Do	26.3.17		Divl. Field Day in training area 8.30 to 6.4	39 621
Do	27.3.17		Bde Field Day in training area 8.30 to 6.4. CAPT J. W.B. TARLETON M.C. joined and took C.2.S. but taken over temp. command of H.Q. in the absence of CAPT. GUN CURRINGTON. M.C. at 4th Army School. 2/LTs J.J. ROGERS(2), A.J. McCANN(Y), D.P. WAGNER (w) and H.M. BLAKE (w) joined. Draft of 13 O.R. joined	44 634
Do	28.3.17		Coy parades including practice with rifle grenades.	44 634
Do	29.3.17		Left BELLOY at 0830 and marched to SOUES (10 miles) which was reached by 1300. H.Q., W & X Coys billeted in SOUEL, Y & Z Coys in CROUY, a village a mile distant. 6 O.R. to Hos. 10.R. transferred to 5th Field Survey Coy.	44 627
SOUES	30.3.17		Left SOUES at 0855 and marched to HALLOY (12 miles) which was reached by 1315. Draft of 43 O.R. joined 29.3.17	44 670
HALLOY	31.3.17		Inspections during the morning.	44 670

H. L. Ridley Lieut
(a/s) I. R. Dub. Fus.
31.3.17

Confidential

War Diary
1st Royal Dublin Fusrs.

For the month of
April 1917

Volume 26

WAR DIARY or INTELLIGENCE SUMMARY

Army Form C. 2118.

Place	Date	Hour	Summary of Events and Information	Remarks and references to Appendices
				Effective S.O. / O.R.
HALLOY LES PERNOIS	1.4.17		2/Lt. J.C. DEVOY took over duties of Acting Adjutant from Lt. H.L. RIDLEY, M.C. Battn. left HALLOY at 11.45 and marched to LONGUEVILLETTE (8 miles) which was reached by 15.30. Lt. A. DALTON transferred to R.E. 2/Lt E.H. ROBERTSON invalided to ENGLAND 21.3.17	42 670
LONGUEVILLETTE	2.4.17		Left LONGUEVILLETTE at 09.00 and marched to BEAUREPAIRE which was reached by 12.00. Billets not very good. Draft of 50 O.R. joined 14 O.R. B.O.R. sent to Cavalry Base.	42 667
BEAUREPAIRE	3.4.17		Parades for training 9-1 and 2-4.30	42 667
BEAUREPAIRE	4.4.17		Coy's trained for training. 1 gun - 1 hour. - 2 pm - 4.30 pm. Draft of 38 O.R. joined. Draft of 50 O.R. joined & Lieut. E.A. SEALE and 2nd Lieut. F.E. LEE joined & posted to Coys. Lieut. G.H. CHANDLER, 2nd Lieut. E.A. SEALE and 2nd Lieut. F.E. LEE joined & posted.	45 793
BEAUDRICOURT	5.4.17		Battn. moved from BEAUREPAIRE to BEAUDRICOURT (8½ miles). Billets fair. Brags of 119 O.R. arrived and posted.	45.- 822.
-"-	6.4.17		Company parades for training. 11 Officers & 135 O.R. sent to ST. POL	45.- 787.
-"-	7.4.17		Company formed to training. Special contact patrol exercise with aeroplane to synchronise.	45.- 787
BAVINCOURT	8.4.17		Battn. marches from BEAUDRICOURT to BAVINCOURT which it reaches at 1/pm. 45.- Billets in huts. R.Sgt.Major BERRILL & 7 O.R. to Base, 20 O.R. to Div. Res. Cy. on A.D.M.S. recommendation.	45.- 813.

WAR DIARY
or
INTELLIGENCE SUMMARY.

(Erase heading not required.)

Army Form C. 2118.

Place	Date	Hour	Summary of Events and Information	Remarks and references to Appendices
	April 1917		(Continued)	
BAVINCOURT	9/10/17		Weather very cold. Company prepare for training. Received orders at 6 p.m. to move.	Sphe. Appx. 45 - 821
	10/4		Company prepare for training. Still under new know but nothing definite.	
SIMONCOURT	11/4		Weather very cold. Battn. moves to SIMONCOURT. Marching very difficult owing to heavy snowfall on bad roads. Billeted in huts.	45 - 813 &c
				45 - 747
ARRAS	12/4		Battn. move from SIMONCOURT to ARRAS. Billets in CITADELLE. Received orders to go into line tomorrow. 10% of strength to remain behind as reinforcements.	45 - 775
	13/4		Battn. parade at 6.45 a.m. and marched to trenches old German front line. Battn. H.Q. + Company H.Q. in good dug outs. Men in shelters. No raids in any depth dug outs.	45 - 860
	14/4		Battn. moves up about 800x to a line opposite TILLOY. Men dig in as trench a couple of hours when orders received to move to BROWN LINE at German new counter attacking village of MONCHY le PREUX. Move across country to new line in Artillery Formation but were not needed on arrival. Consolidate defences of ORANGE HILL + trench down there.	45 - 780
ORANGE HILL	15/4		Out working party of all available O.R. to restore defences of MONCHY to A1 communication trench. Battn. Leaves at 9 p.m. Raining heavily during night. 10 O.R. wounded during	45 - 779

WAR DIARY or INTELLIGENCE SUMMARY

Army Form C. 2118.

For month of APRIL 1917.

Place	Date	Hour	Summary of Events and Information	Remarks and references to Appendices
				EFFECTIVE STRENGTH. Offrs. OR.
ORANGE HILL	16/4		Working party of last night returned at 1am. They got heavily shelled and lost 5 OR. Killed and 31 OR. wounded. Owing to heavy shell fire and heavy rain the work could not be completed. Owing to party having to scatter there were several OR missing – they eventually returned.	45. 743.
"	17/4		Working party again goes out tonight at 9pm. to complete work. Working party returns at 6.30am. Heavily shelled again and 8 OR missing, believed wounded. 2nd.Lt. 8. BAKER wounded by H.E. In evening whole leaving ORANGE HILL defences. Received orders for move to MONCHY tomorrow.	44. 734.
FIRING LINE MONCHY.	18/4		Relieved by Composite Battn. ESSEX-NEWFOUNDLAND at 9pm and Battn. moved to MONCHY + relieves LANCS. FUS. W. X. Y. Coys. in line. Z Coy. in reserve. Battn. HQ billets in old German dugout. Village incessantly shelled and extremely dangerous to move about above ground. There are an extraordinary number of dead cavalry horses and men strewn in the streets but it is impossible to bury them. 1 OR. repair home stay.	44. 735.
"	19/4		Enemy still heavily shelling - 6 OR. + 2 Lt. Col. KIDSON wounded. Nothing else of interest. Grave of 17 OR. Louis details at ARRAS	43. 856
"	20/4		Shell heavily shelled. Several O.R. of Reserve Coy. buried 2 OR killed 10 OR. wounded One OR. accidentally shot by sniper of ours. 2/Lt. J.C. DEVOY wounded also Capt. F.S. LANIGAN-OKEEFFE wounded	41. 841

Army Form C. 2118.

WAR DIARY
or
INTELLIGENCE SUMMARY.
(Erase heading not required.)

Instructions regarding War Diaries and Intelligence Summaries are contained in F. S. Regs., Part II. and the Staff Manual respectively. Title pages will be prepared in manuscript.

For month of APRIL 1917.

Place	Date	Hour	Summary of Events and Information	Remarks and references to Appendices
Henri Levi				EFFEC. 85 Off. OR.
MONCHY.	21/4		Battn. relieved by LANCS. FUS. at 9pm. Relief complete by 12mn. Battn. arrive in ARRAS at 4.30am. Billeted in Cavalry Lost & damp. Total casualties to day	41 - 829.
			7 OR. killed & 5 OR. wounded. Details from ST. POL arrive.	
ARRAS.	22/4		Companies reorganise after heavy losses noted.	41 - 829.
ORANGE HILL	23/4		Battn. moves up to BROWN LINE at 4.30am. That night take over section defences of MONCHY from 2 Companies of K.O.S.B. Orders issued for general attack tomorrow evening.	
Henri Levi MONCHY	24/4		Lt. W.C. DEVOY rejoins from 7th Durhams. 4 OR. wounded. 1 OR. missing. Major H.C.C. CROZIER M.C. joins Battn. to assist hold 0.2.1.8.5. at 4pm. However army orders for general attack cancelled at 11pm. Battn. to assault hill 0.2.1.8.5. at 4pm. However did not arrive & Brigade runner losing his way others regarding change in line of barrage (undertaken) by our artillery) with great gallantry, and went face in very heavy shell machine gun and rifle fire. After stubborn resistance they were compelled to fall back on our original front line leaving 10 Officers (Lt. BYRNE) & 190 R. killed, 5 Officers (Lieuts. TOOTH REILLY, BARRY, HEGARTY & ROGERS) & 55 OR. wounded and 37 missing in Nomansland. Owing to these being no artillery support the last attack by the Battn. was unsuccessful. W.D.	43 - 824. 37 - 713

WAR DIARY or INTELLIGENCE SUMMARY

Army Form C. 2118.

Month of April 1917

Place	Date	Hour	Summary of Events and Information	Remarks and references to Appendices
ARRAS	25/4		Battn. relieved in trenches by 1st GORDONS. Arrive in ARRAS at about 5 am where they are billeted in the RUE PASTEUR. Rest until 6pm then move to BERNEVILLE in busses. Very comfortably billeted in huts. 2nd Lt HAGERTY taken on strength +10 R.	38. 727.
DANQUETIN	26/4		Battn moves to WANQUETIN. Men billeted in huts - baths available. 2/Lt. G.P. O'SULLIVAN invalided to ENGLAND. Company re-organise.	37. 726.
SOUASTRE	27/4		Battn. marches to SOUASTRE - 11 miles out - have long halt in midday meal. Men billeted in huts. Companies to start re-organising at once if to remain here for a couple of days.	37. 716.
"	28/4		Company re-organising + General Spring-up. Casualty returns Inspection of arms and equipment etc. Draft of 1 officer (2/Lt MASON) + 12 O.R. 3 O.R. from Hospital	37. 741.
"	29/4		Church Service to all ranks	37. 741.
"	30/4		Companies parade for training - dinners out. Weather remains fine. 2/Lt I.D. MAC-KENZIE takes over duties of Transport Officer vice 2/Lt A. HOLMAN R.A.M.C.	37. 741.

CONFIDENTIAL.

WAR   DIARY

1ST ROYAL DUBLIN FUSILIERS

MAY, 1917.

(Volume XXVII)

WAR DIARY / INTELLIGENCE SUMMARY

Army Form C. 2118.

1st R. DUB FUS.

Summary of Events and Information — Month of May 1917.

Place	Date	Hour	Summary of Events and Information	Remarks and references to Appendices
GOUY-en-ARTOIS	1/5		March from SOUASTRE to GOUY-en-ARTOIS where Battn. went into huts.	Sh.51.c Off.G2
ARRAS	2/5		Battn. marched from GOUY-en-ARTOIS to ARRAS. Arrived at 11 p.m. Were billeted in SCHRAMM Cavalry Bks. Officers in town.	35 - 667
"	3/5		Battn. standing by throughout at one hour's notice. Town shelled at intervals during the afternoon – no casualties in Bn. Bnght of 10 Officers (Lt SOMERS) & 130 O.R. joined Battn. under shorl notice from one Corps, and parties to RITZ DUMP to take 300s of Canadian wire. Enemy shelling sets fire to by ammunition dump on Canal bank.	35 - 667 36 - 745
"	4/5		Also a horse to rear of N. Coy billets – N. of BARRACKS. No casualties in the Battn. Company training. The Bn. had been allotted the RACECOURSE and old ENGLISH trench S. of CAMBRAI Rd. on alternate days.	H.Q.R.15 Regt 36. 745 731
"	5/5 6/5		Company training. Billets shelled at intervals – no casualties. W.SOMERS joined. Company training. 5 Officers [Capt. GUN-CUNNINGHAME, 2/Lt. MAUNSELL, 2/Lt. JONES-NOWLAN,	36.#H
"	7/5		2/Lt CONERNEY, 2/Lt WALKER] joined & 8 O.R. 158 wounded by shell-fire whilst on duty at Barrack Gate.	40 - 735
"	8/5		Weather changed – very wet. Companies trained indoors.	40 - 735

WAR DIARY
or
INTELLIGENCE SUMMARY.
(Erase heading not required.)

Army Form C. 2118.

Instructions regarding War Diaries and Intelligence Summaries are contained in F. S. Regs., Part II. and the Staff Manual respectively. Title pages will be prepared in manuscript.

MAY — continued 1917.

Place	Date	Hour	Summary of Events and Information	Remarks and references to Appendices
ARRAS	9/5		Battn. moves from SCHRAMM BARRACKS to MUSEUM CELLARS owing to former place been borrowed. Usual Coy. parade for training in afternoon. 1 Officer (Lt. LEE) invalided to ENGLAND — 2 O.R. accidentally wounded — ammunition in haversacks.	After Ref. STR OR 39 – 733
-"-	10/5		Battn. goes out to Northern slope of ORANGE HILL at 9 p.m. and digs 3 Strong Points. Shelled at intervals during the night – no casualties – work completed.	39 – 733
BERNEVILLE	11/5		Move from ARRAS to BERNEVILLE — men billeted in barns and officers in huts, hospital.	
-"-			Extremely warm and quite a number of men fell out on the march. 9 O.R. reported to Hospital and Officer posted to ST. POL. (2/Lt. P.A. ROBINSON.)(Lt. HOLLON rejoined from leave.)	40 – 742
-"-	12/5		Coys. parade for training, also night operations. 40 O.R. evacuated, 25 O.R. to ENGLAND.	40. 736
-"-	13/5		Church Parade for all religions. Practice night attack — usual Stand To & Coy. Drills.	40. 736
-"-	14/5		Coys. parade for training known as Trench Baths. in afternoon. 5 O.R. evacuated.	40. 731.
ARRAS	15/5		Bn. marches from BERNEVILLE to ARRAS and is billeted in GRAND PLACE — in cellars.	
-"-	16/5		Found carrying party of 2 Offs. + 146 O.R. to Bn. to LA FOSSE FARM.	40. 731.
-"-	17/5		Training on RACECOURSE. Again furnish carrying party as before. 4 O.R. to Base. Re. Cpy. Owing to inclement weather, Companies have indoors. Firework carrying party to LIEVENS PROJECTORS. 2 O.R. missing.	40. 740.

Army Form C. 2118

WAR DIARY or INTELLIGENCE SUMMARY

(Erase heading not required.)

For month of MAY 1917.

Place	Date	Hour	Summary of Events and Information	Remarks and references to Appendices
ARRAS.	18/5		Companies to RACECOURSE to bathing. LT. CHANDLER to Hospital. 2 OR. evacuated.	40 - 738.
—"—	19/5		Companies to CITADELLE to bathing. Under 1 hours notice to move to the trenches	
			87TH Bde. attack INFANTRY HILL at 9pm. Shells in ARRAS - no casualties.	
			LIEUT. LETCHWORTH joined at ST. POL. 1OR. to 4th. F.Survey Coy. R.E. 2 OR. wounded.	40. 731.
—"—	20/5		Relieve Middx. Regt in BROWN LINE. 34 OR. evacuated to hospital.	41. 697.
BROWN LINE	21/5		Batn. finds working parties (wiring) S. of MONCHY, at night.	41. 697.
	22/5		Batn. again wiring as last night. 1 OR. wounded. 1 OR. dies of wounds.	41. 695.
—"—	23/5		Bn. relieve LANCS. FUS. at MONCHY LE PREUX - Left sector Northern end.	41. 693.
—"—	24/5		Bn. digging line - improving trenches - wiring at night. 1 OR. wounded. 16 OR. to Base Depot B.	41. 708.
—"—	25/5		Bn. working as before. No casualties.	41. 708.
—"—	26/5		Bn. working as before. Capt. Gen. CUNNINGHAME M.C. & 2/Lt. HERNON wounded. 1 OR. killed. 3 OR. wounded.	39. 704.
—"—	27/5		Bn. working in trenches. Parties tee'd off to bury dead which were lying about. Lt. JONES-NOWLAN	38. 704.
—"—	28/5		Bn. improving French trenches - wiring. 2 OR. killed. 1 OR. to ENGLAND (Commission Australian) 1 OR. Shock	
			Att. as above. 2/Lt. GIBBONS joined at ST. POL.	39. 690.
	29/5		Owing to casualties in officers, some temporary transfers have been necessary. 2/Lt. McINTYRE takes X Coy.	20R. wounded 39. 688.
	30/5		Weather breaks. Very heavy rain - trenches flooded. LANCS. FUS. & MIDDX. Regt. attack.	
	31/5		in rgt. Retaliatory barrage wounds 7 OR. 1 OR. killed. 6 OR. to Base.	

1875 Wt. W592/826 1,000,000 4/15 J.B.C. & A. A.D.S.S./Forms/C. 2118.

1st Bn, Royal Dublin Fusiliers.
War Diary for month of June
1917.
Volume No,27.

Army Form C. 2118

WAR DIARY
or
INTELLIGENCE SUMMARY
(Erase heading not required.)

Instructions regarding War Diaries and Intelligence Summaries are contained in F.S. Regs., Part II. and the Staff Manual respectively. Title Pages will be prepared in manuscript.

Summary of Events and Information: Month of May 1917.

Place	Date	Hour	Summary of Events and Information	Remarks and references to Appendices
HONCOURT	3/6		Bn. adjourned to 2 S.W. B. in the line – relief complete 3.45 am. 7 O.R. Killed 11 O.R. wounded	39. 673
ARRAS	—		Bn. Billets in GRANDE PLACE – Billets comfortable.	39. 673
BERNEVILLE	2/6		Bn. marches to BERNEVILLE – accommodations in barns. 2 officers & some 10 O.R. rejoined by troop	39. 674
BERNOIS	3/6		Bn. entrains at BAUMETZ for CANDAS then marches to PERNOIS. Billets in barns	
"	4/6		Huts. Lights down by 9.30 pm. 4 Killingly struck off nom.	40. 674
"	4/6		Company training & inspections. 10 O.R. joined at St Pol. 10 O.R. to BASE	40. 683
"	5/6		Company training. Special attention being given to Musketry. 14 O.R. to Hospital	40. 669
"	6/6		Company Training – 1 officer & 2 N.C.O's per Company commenced 3 day course on Physical Training, Bayonet fighting and Special Instructors attached for one week. Re Brigade Draft – 79 O.R. joined at St Pol	40. 776
"	7/6		Company training. From St Pol the following join Batt. Lieut G.H. CHANDLER "W" Coy who had been in Hospital, 2nd Lt. W.M. GIBBINS posted to Z Coy 2 Lt H.H. LETCHWORTH posted to Y Coy + 145 O.R.	40. 748
"	8/6		Company training – Special lecture in afternoon on Anti gas measures by Div. Anti gas Instructor to officers & N.C.O's. Draft joined 6 O.R.	40. 748
"	9/6		Company training – Lecture by Commanding officer & demonstration "new formation of Company in attack" all officers & N.C.O's present. In afternoon Batta. beat 86 Bde T.M.B. at football 6 goals to 2. Weather very fine. Inspection of billets, Rifles & equipment, Transport by Comdg. officer E.u.	40. 754
"	10/6		Entertainment by own Concert Party in the evening. Draft – 173 O.R. joined Church Service for all Religions –	40. 927

1875. Wt. W593/826 1,000,000 4/15 J.B.C. & A. A.D.S.S./Forms/C. 2118.

WAR DIARY / INTELLIGENCE SUMMARY

Army Form C. 2118

Place	Date	Hour	Summary of Events and Information	Remarks and references to Appendices
PERNOIS	11th		For month of June 1917. Company training - a 6 day course in field engineering for all subaltern officers & 3 N.C.O.'s per company commenced under R.E. Instructors. Companies firing on the Ranges(no) which have been fitted up with Moving & disappearing targets etc & fall-plates by the Pioneers.	
"	12th		Capt. W.P. OULTON M.C. & 2/Lieut. T.H. LADDIS rejoin from Hospital. Battalion route march in the morning - Specialist training in the afternoon	40.927.
"	13th		Capt. C.W. MOFFATT to Instructional staff XVIII Corps Infantry School & 2.O.R. to Lewis gun school. Company training. 2nd Lieut. g SOMERS & 23.O.R. proceed to be attached to Kent Field Coy R.E. for training in Tunnelled Dug Out Construction	39.925.
"	14th		Company training - 2/Lt. C.J. G. COVERNEY admitted to Hospital. 2.O.R. from Hospital	39.925.
"	15th		Company training. Major L.M. Browne & 2 Lt. P. LAFFAN (posted to X coy) joined	39.927.
"	16th		6 O.R. transferred to Labour Corps, 1 O.R. to Hospital, 1 O.R. to Base Inf'd. Company training - Divisional Horse show held at GORGES. Transport sergeants horse awarded 2nd Prize in Brigade Competition - Draft 7.O.R. joined. 1 O.R. to Hospital.	41.919.
"	17th		Church services for all denominations. 4.O.R. rejoined from Hospital	41.926
"	18th		Company training - 2nd Lt. A.V. HASTINGS posted to Y Coy & 2nd Lt. A.G. SIDWELL posted to W Coy joined - R.S.M. CULLEN.P.T. granted a Permanent Commission & ordered to join 8th Batt. R.D.F. as.	41-930
"	19th		Company training. 3. O.R. rejoined from Hospital	43.929
"	20th		Commenced three company training in the morning - In the afternoon Sports for exception of the high jump & also the Special Prize presented by the G. Instructor by the G.O.C. Brigade for the 2 Smartest men "Full Marching Order", 2 men per	43.932.

Army Form C. 2118

WAR DIARY
or
INTELLIGENCE SUMMARY
(Erase heading not required.)

Instructions regarding War Diaries and Intelligence Summaries are contained in F.S. Regs., Part II. and the Staff Manual respectively. Title Pages will be prepared in manuscript.

Place	Date	Hour	Summary of Events and Information — June 1917	Remarks and references to Appendices
PERNOIS	20th	continued	Company training. Draft 11 O.R. joined, 1 O.R. to 35th Light Rly. Operating Coy. 1 O.R. to BASE under age	43.941
"	21st		Brigade Tactical Scheme carried out by all units of the 86th Brigade. Divisional General, g.O.C. & O.S.C. units in 87th & 88th Brigades present. 2 O.R. killed in action & 2 O.R. wounded in action 17-6-17 whilst attached Town Commandant ARRAS. 2 D.R. to Hospital	43.935
"	22nd		Brigade Route march in the morning – In the afternoon Specialist Training. 2nd Lt. T.H.L. ADDIS admitted to Hospital	43.935
"	23rd		Company training in the morning. Most successful Battalion Boxing Competition held in the afternoon. The majority of winners came from W. Company – 2/Lt. W.M. GIBBINS admitted to Hospital. 1 O.R. from	43.935
"	24th		Church Service for all denominations – Hospital returned	43.936
"	25th		Battalion route march in safety morning. "A" officers & N.C.O.'s available witness a Demonstration by 86th Bde T.M.B. 8 officers & 8 N.C.O.'s attend Demonstration in attack at 3rd Army school AUXI-LE-CHATEAU – Specialist Training in afternoon – Major A. MOORE D.S.O. & 2/Lt E. HAWTREY (posted to Z Coy) joined, 1 O.R. to H.Q.I.E. & 4.O.R. to A.P.M. 29th Divn. 4 O.R. to BASE "under age", 2 O.R. to Hospital	45.925
"	26th		Company training in the morning – Cleaning up billets preparatory to move in the afternoon.	45.925
"	27		March to Candas where Battalion less X (oy) entrain at 3.20 pm – Dinners served before reaching station – Batt. detrain at 12 Midnight & march to near HERINGE in PROVEN areas where Coy. are accommodated in Tents	

WAR DIARY or INTELLIGENCE SUMMARY

Army Form C. 2118

(Erase heading not required.)

For month of June 1917

Place	Date	Hour	Summary of Events and Information	Remarks and references to Appendices
PERNOIS	27th		Continued and Burrows except of "W" Coy who have a burn - Settled down by 4.30AM. X Coy lined by late 10am + on arrival ac settled down by 6.45AM. 1.OR [No 9569 Pte Higgins] shot himself, believed suicide.	45. 921.
BOVENACKERS	28th		Showery - 3 OR to Hospital, 1 OR to hospital. Inside continues showery. Men spend day resting + attending to proper arrangement in Billets. 1 OR returned from Hospital. Draft 2/Lt G.H. NOBLETT joined proto X Coy	46. 922
"	29th		Inspections, Drill, repeated trainings. No training area available - Draft 17 OR joined, 3 OR to Hospital wounded, 1 OR accidentally wounded, 1 OR to Hospital. 1 OR returned from Hospital	46. 935
"	30th		Battalion route march - Very hot day. 1 OR returned from hospital, Lieut H.G. AYLMER joined.	47. 935.

Vol 16

"WAR DIARY"
of
"1st Royal Dublin Fusiliers"
for Month of
July 1917
Volume 28.

15 X
7 sheets

WAR DIARY or INTELLIGENCE SUMMARY

Army Form C. 2118.

(Erase heading not required.)

For the month of July 1917.

Place	Date	Hour	Summary of Events and Information	Remarks and references to Appendices
PROVEN areas	1st		Church Services for all Denominations	
—	2nd		Company Specialist Training. 2 OR to Hospital. 46R Taken on establishment of 183 Tunnel Coy R.E.	47 - 935.
—	3rd		Major General Sir Beauvoir DeLISLE held a Regt. Inspection of Bn H.Qrs. for O.C. Batt & Companies Officer Bde — Specialist Training. 2nd Lt T.H.L. ADDIS invalided to England. 2nd Lt A.V.G. KILLINGLEY & 13 OR attacked 85th T.M. Battery are shown off strength. Strength 3 OR joined	47 - 929. 45 - 919.
—	4th		Batt proceeded to Training Area. Lent by guards Division for Training.	45 - 919. No 60 Yper
Belgium 28 N.W. Ypres Edn SIA	5th		Batt move forward into Support. W, Y & part of X Coy conveyed in Lorries remainder of Batt march — on arrival W Coy supply working party, Y Coy doing M.G. Sam's mit infil	
A 10 d "IN A WOOD"			All ranks very comfortable in bunkers Huts situated in a wood — Belgian orderly were received in occupation hut — Batt will have to find working parties total 480 O.R. each 24 hours — Weather very fine. 2/Lt W.P. KINNEEN to R.E. Corps on probation working parties supplied for 458th Field Rich Heavy Regt Coy R.E. & Heavy artillary groups	44 - 919.
—	6th		Remainder of Batt clean up Camp. 10 O.R. from Hospital 5 O.R. to Hospital	44 - 915.
—	7th		Batt engaged as yesterday 1 O.R. to Hospital	44 - 914.
—	8th		Batt find working parties as before. Church Services for all denominations. 1 O.R. reported from Hospital	44 - 915.

Army Form C. 2118.

WAR DIARY
or
INTELLIGENCE SUMMARY.
(Erase heading not required.)

For month of July 1917.

Place	Date	Hour	Summary of Events and Information	Remarks and references to Appendices
Belgium 28/NW Edition 5A "A 10 d" "IN A WOOD"	9th	9 a.m.	Batt. furnished working Parties as before & clean up Camp. 2 OR wounded - map of H.C. CROZIER M.C. attached to 16th MIDDLESEX REGt - Weather Wet.	43.913
"	10th		Batt. fnsd. working Parties as before. Raiding Parties 1 officer & 30 men per Coy parade in town each day for instruction under Major MOORE D.S.O. 1 OR to Hospital	43.912
"	11th		Working parties as before - Lieut A.G. AYLMER transferred to 2nd Batt. 3 OR to Hospital	42.909
"	12th		This Camp now officially named DUBLIN CAMP. Batt. moves up the line to relieve 1st NEWFOUNDLAND. REGt on CANAL BANK [BELGIUM Sheet 28 N.W. B24 + 9.b] W + X Coys + 1 Platoon of Z. lay preced the Batt hading by Motor lorries as far as BRIELEN. Jm Thilgan engaged in carrying Ammunition & gas cylinders from MARENGO H.Q. along Canal Bank. Remainder of Batt. Holg.b., Y + balance of Z. lay move of about 7.45 P.M. - Relief complete at 12.30 A.M. W + X Coys + Platoon of Z. of from Batt. which was in support about 1 A.M. 1st NFLD. raised Enemy at 2 A.M., but found trenches empty - Batt. details move to "A" Camp (A9. d9.4). 2nd Lt H.M. BLAKE & 3 OR wounded, 1 OR to BASE hospt., 1 OR to 86 3rd H.Qt.5, 1 OR returned from Hospital	41.905
CANAL BANK B24.d 9.b (Belgium Sheet 28/N.W.)	13th		BATT. relieve 2nd HAMPSHIRE REGt in FRONT LINE [left of ZWAANHOF Sec Dr] Relief commenced about 2 P.M. Coy H.Qs. at 5:15 p.m. - Order ZTY in front line	

WAR DIARY
or
INTELLIGENCE SUMMARY.

Army Form C. 2118.

(Erase heading not required.)

Summary of Events and Information for MONTH of JULY 1917

Place	Date	Hour	Summary of Events and Information	Remarks and references to Appendices
CANAL BANK P24. 6.9.6. [Belgium 28 N.W.] [Batt. Hdqts.]	13th	(Continued)	On left, right repeated. X Coy & 1 platoon of W in support. W Coy less 1 platoon in Reserve. Front line held by "POSTS" - carrying parties, ration parties, genls. sent up of W & X coys. Strength.	
"	14th		Intermittent Artillery during night. DETAILS supply working parties. Enemy artillery quieter. Support trenches coming on for a good deal of attention. Lewis guns of W coy Knocked out - CANAL BANK Shelled regularly. Genl. de Lisle goes round front line system - Gas sent over by LIEVENS Projectors - 3 O.R. killed 5 O.R. Wounded	41 - 905 41. 897
"	15th		Heavy bombardment of Enemy line by our Heavy guns, for 3 hours. Some of them fire very short. In the evening they are again short, one of our own 6" shells killing Capt. H.L. RIDLEY M.C. (in command of Y coy) at 9 P.M. - 4 O.R's killed by Enemy shell fire, 4 O.R wounded, 1 O.R died of wounds.	40. 888.
"	16th		Front trenches classed by us for bombardment of Enemy lines - guns were firing continuously - Batt. Hdqts. heavily shelled. 2 O.R's killed, 7 O.R wounded 1 O.R accidentally wounded - 2nd Lt. N.M. GIBBINS invalided to England.	39 - 878.
"	17th		Batt. relieved in FRONT line by 1st LANCASHIRE. FUS. and returns to CANAL BANK in Support. Batt. Hdqts. attending Nuisance. 1. O.R to BASE under age. 1 O.R rejoined from Hospital - 12 O.R to Evacuated to Hospital	39. 866

WAR DIARY
or
INTELLIGENCE SUMMARY.
(Erase heading not required.)

Army Form C. 2118.

Place	Date	Hour	Summary of Events and Information	Remarks and references to Appendices
CANAL BANK B+ 4.9.6 (3rd Gwent Sheet 28 NW) Batt HQ.	18th		Batt. busy in support finding working parties day & night. 100 OR's carrying for Bde H.Q.T. 40 OR's for LANC. Fus. also 100 OR's digging HARDEN Trench for 16th MIDDLESEX Regt.	
			Heavy Enemy Barrage all roads on front & support lines from 11 P.M. & about 1 A.M. on 19th inst — 3 OR's killed, 7 OR wounded. 2 OR's & England candidates for commissions	39.854
" —	19th		Batt relieved in support line by 16th Ry. W. Fus. (38th Div) relief completed by 12.30 am — Batt returns to camps on CROMBEKE — POPERINGHE Road (about 2 miles short of the former) all in about 6 am 20th inst. DETAILS furnishing 30 OR of W Coy under 2/Lt R. MAGUIRE — a RAIDING Party, who are having out of the line & ready in case the Batt were asked to make a RAID) proceeded to this	
CAMP CROMBEKE	20th		Camps from H Camps early in the afternoon — 1 OR to hospital Men spend day resting.	39.853
POPERINGE ROAD	21st		Inspections. Cleaning up camps which was in a very dirty condition.	39.853
" —	22nd		Church services held in camps for all denominations. 1 O.R L.	
			England on transfer to ½ Commission. 1 OR to Prison. 1 OR reported from Hospital	39.852
" —	23		Company training 1 OR to Hospital 1 OR from Hospital	39.852
" —	24		Batt moves to Camps Proven Area No 3 — Tents & Shelters 72 Farm Hands to Base undergo	39.851

2/Lt A.G. SIDWELL & 30 OR go as Working Party to 23rd H.A. Group —

WAR DIARY
or
INTELLIGENCE SUMMARY.
(Erase heading not required.)

Army Form C. 2118.

Month of **July 1917**

Place	Date	Hour	Summary of Events and Information	Remarks and references to Appendices
Camps PROVEN AREA No 3	25th		Batt. less details [to be left behind in view of coming operations] marched off at 4.30 am to Training ground at HERZEELE for Brigade Field day. It commenced to rain very heavily at 8 am but cleared shortly after 1 pm. Batt. returns to camp at 5 PM. C.S.M. WALLIS commissioned remaining in Batt. posted to X Corps Hospital.	40 & 9
	26th		Company training. To thegn at 2 R. To T.M. Bty. 1 R, 5 OR Recpt Corps Depot	40 851
	27th		Batt. less Details marched off at 8.15 am to Training ground at HERZEELE for Batt. field day – Return to camp about 5 PM. Very warm day. 1 OR wounded	
	28th		1 OR reported. 2/Lt. C.T. CARROLL joined posted to B Coy. 2/Lt. B. BLAYLOCK joined at 29th Own Depot Batt. Company training – 2 OR wounded. 1 OR sick in C.C.S.	42 851 42 852
	29th		Church service. All denominations. Very wet from 10 am until shortly after 2 pm. Boxing competition for the men held at 5.30 pm. Very good fights. Batt. less 2 100% details (who remain to move 31st) went to 29th Own Depot Batt. XIV Corps Reinforcement Camps	42 852 42 852
	30th		Company training inspections in the morning.	
			BOLLEZEELE; remaining 2 10% details plus Administrative staff move with Batt, but will remain with Transport Lines when Batt. go up into action) move at 11.25 pm to Camp Proven 2 area sheet 19 BELGIUM X20 d 5.3	

Army Form C. 2118.

WAR DIARY
or
INTELLIGENCE SUMMARY.
(Erase heading not required.)

for Month of July 1917

Place	Date	Hour	Summary of Events and Information	Remarks and references to Appendices
PROVEN AREA No 3	30th		*continued*. This night of 4/7. ZERO hour 3.50 AM morning of 31st July. The 29th Div. are Corps Reserve and are to follow through the Guard's Div. who open the attack on our sector, on their RIGHT are the 1st FRENCH Div. on their LEFT the 38th WELCH Div. we(K?) 20th Div. "Corps Reserve" behind them, forth latter being of the XIV Corps. - The Batt are held in readiness to move at 3 hours notice. - The men are in very good spirits. -	
PROVEN AREA No 2	31st		Very dull rainy day. - Bad for observation. - Rain commencing in the evening continues through night. Bad weather appears to dog all our offensives! 2/Lt JEB MAUNSELL & T.W.H MASON to remain in ENGLAND. On l/t 3.0R joined Div report Batt. 2OR returned from hospital, 1OR Evacuated, 1OR to Base unfit.	40.855

16 X
8 sheets

9.8.17

War Diary
of
1st Bn. Royal Dublin Fusiliers
for
Month of August 1917
Volume 29

Army Form C. 2118.

WAR DIARY
or
INTELLIGENCE SUMMARY.
(Erase heading not required.)

Instructions regarding War Diaries and Intelligence Summaries are contained in F. S. Regs., Part II. and the Staff Manual respectively. Title pages will be prepared in manuscript.

for month of August 1917 -

Place	Date	Hour	Summary of Events and Information	Remarks and references to Appendices
PROVEN AREA No 2.	1st		Very wet day. — To Base under age 1. OR who 1. OR of DURHAM L.INF. who was attached	
BELGIUM Sheet 28 X20 a 53			3. OR warranted 1 OR joined 2g: 10 oyput Batt	40. 857.
" "	2nd		Still raining, continuous wet since evening of 31st July. OR received Batt	
			no longer under 3 hours notice to move. Companies parade under their own commanders. 1 OR warranted. 6. OR to Employment Company	40. 844
" "	3rd		Again very wet. Batt moves to FORREST ENCAMPMENTS [28 N.W BELGIUM A.10.b] close to DUBLIN Camp — C.O 72 1.C in TENTS, other officers then in BWonces, very uncomfortable as no place in so very muddy — 2/Lt AE TELFER granted commission in INDIAN Res Officers proceeded FUK on Embarkation leave — Strength of Batt	39. 844.
FORREST AREA CAMP. 13.	4th		Fine day but overcast. Men engaged in cleaning up Camp 2 OR warranted	39. 934.
" "	5th		90 OR joined at Provonne at Provonne before Batt	
			In the morning Church Service for all denominations. Batt less Details and Admin ishative Staff move to Camp [BELGIUM Sheet 28 N.W] R.Z.f west about 1200 yds	
CAMP, 120 x K	6th		South of WOESTEN — 1 OR Evacuated, 5 OR permanently attached 183 Tunn Cy RE	39. 928
WOESTEN			Transport details etc. move to Camp close to DE WIPPE CABARET + Roads. Batt moves A Coys onto Suffolk Track WHITE HOPE CORNER — BOESINGHE PONTOON	

Army Form C. 2118.

WAR DIARY
or
INTELLIGENCE SUMMARY.
(Erase heading not required.)

for Month of AUGUST 1917

Place	Date	Hour	Summary of Events and Information	Remarks and references to Appendices
Camp B.T.C.	6th		Continued, and relieve 4th GRENADIER GUARDS in left sectr. Batt H.Q. SAULES FARM. Preparation. 2 coy in front support, W coy at SAULES Fm, X coy 1 Platoon ABRI Fm, ½ Platoon MAJOR'S Fm, 1½ Platoon BLUE LINE, Y coy BLUE LINE. 2/Lts J.B. JOHNSTON & W.J. SPEISS joined at DEPOT Batt. Chaplains between Shrub Mc Knight	41-927
SAULES Fm	7th		Shelling of some intensity during day. 2 coy have went completion Batt relieved 4th G.G. in left sectr front line. relief completed by 1.30 am. 86th Bde in structure change scheme of defence, fresh positions have to be dug. W.F.X coys in front line on left respectively, each having a platoon in close support. Y coy in support to those coys. Z coy in Reserve. Batt H.Q at CAPTAINS Fm. Batt suffer many casualties having relief as a ruse for decent enemy had a barrage on approaches to front lines. Draft joined 4 O.R.	41-930
CAPTAINS Fm	8th		Enemy artillery very active. own aeroplanes fly very low over enemy trenches & fire at them. only 1 hostile M.G. known to engage them. Lt. A. CLENDRUM from 13 Ry INNIS KILLING Fus joined & remains with Dr Cards.	42-93D
— " —	9th		In the early hours W coy pushed out a Patrol over the STEENBEEK to reconnoitre ground NE of bridge at W20 d 76 [LANGEMARCK Sheet Edition 2 1/10 000] Same coy establish	

Army Form C. 2118.

WAR DIARY
or
INTELLIGENCE SUMMARY.
(Erase heading not required.)

Place	Date	Hour	Summary of Events and Information AUGUST 1919	Remarks and references to Appendices
CAPTAINS Fm	9th	to hunk of	A post SE of same bridge across the river. This post was taken by itself was for the day. X toy fail to establish a post at PASSERELLE Fm which is found strongly held by M.G. snipers. Enemy artillery shelled exceedingly active - Continued shelling of post by Lyddite Mornings High ex- SENTIER Fm, FOURCHE Fm CAPTAINS Fm - Pte understood Batth established 3 posts on E bank of STEENBEEK W Coy maintain their first post opposite Zonnebeck - recover post on E bank about 100 x to the SE of first post. X Coy again fail to establish their post at PASSERELLE Fm. In accordance with orders from Bde Coy establish posts	
			prior to our withdrawn at 1.30 a.m. The Batt is relieved by 16th MIDDLESEX Regt in front line. Relief complete 1.30 A.M Batt return to Camp at B.2.c.1. Casualties 1 OR killed, 1 OR died of wounds, 2 Lieutenants, 38 OR wounded. 1 Reaming part unit 1 OR.	42-890
P.T.C. (BRANDHOEK 28 N.W.)	10th		Batt move at 2 pm to Camp at DE WIPPE from Rumah - Accomodation Huts Very comfortable. 1 OR refused Major F.A. WILSON to 11th Batt CHESHIRE Reft as 2nd in comd - 7 OR wounded.	41-886
DE WIPPE CAMP	11th		Reorganization Manouerres - Draft 5 OR joined Depot Batt. 1 OR & Hospital 1 OR from Evacuated	41-888

WAR DIARY or INTELLIGENCE SUMMARY

Army Form C. 2118.

Summary of Events and Information AUGUST 1917

Place	Date	Hour	Summary of Events and Information	Remarks and references to Appendices
Camp DE WIPPE	12"		Church Service for all denominations — Concert for the men in the evening	
"	13"		1 O.R. to Base Depot.	41-889
"	"		Company Training & Inspections. 5 O.R. evacuated. S.O.R. attached 86" M.G. Coy missing.	
"	14"		Organisation etc of Companies — Batt moves at 8.45 p.m. to Camps B.7.C. [ETON CAMP] all in Issued down by 9-30 p.m. 2 O.R. evacuated	41-879
ETON CAMP	15"		Batt leaves camp at 8.30 p.m. moves up - enters CANAL at CRAPOUILLOT PONTOON	41-877
B.7.C.			Takes up position in WOOD 15. Attack by 29" Div (87" + 88" Bde.) ZERO 4-45 a.m. 16" Inst. 86" Bde 7 1st INNISKILLING Bns in Reserve.	
LANNES F^m	16"		at 11 a.m whilst attack was in progress Batt marches to front - line relieves 4 WORCESTER Rgt	41-877
N.17.A.2.3			who are consolidating 3rd objective - Batt in B. Sect. R. INNISK Ins on left	
SAULES F^m			At night Batt moves up to front-line relieves 4 WORCESTER Rgt who are consolidating 3rd objective - Batt in B. Sect. R. INNISK Ins on left	
~~SCHREIBOEK~~ PROEMBEEK F.M. N.10.B10			2nd Rgt Inn on Right - Batt. H.Q. at CANNES F. Reported no Hospital 2 O.R.	41-879
"	17"		A fairly quiet day. Enemy put 4 coys in front our lines heavy casualties. X by fire on enemy patrol of 3 who surrender. They belong to 119 Inf Regt 26 Divs — 2nd Lt HAWTREY on patrol meets an enemy patrol of 3, fires on them, 2 escape. I surrenders. Another of the enemy on nearing his lines surrenders to our X coy.	41-879

Army Form C. 2118.

WAR DIARY
or
INTELLIGENCE SUMMARY.
(Erase heading not required.)

Instructions regarding War Diaries and Intelligence Summaries are contained in F.S. Regs., Part II. and the Staff Manual respectively. Title pages will be prepared in manuscript.

Place	Date	Hour	Summary of Events and Information	Remarks and references to Appendices
			AUGUST 1917	
CANNES Fm	18th		Shelling become heavy during open registering very accurately on front line H.Q, two direct hits by 5.9 Hows on latter. 2nd Lt HAWTREY wounded 17th inst.	40.879
— " —	19th		Morning & part afternoon shelling fairly heavy, a lull in the evening. Draft 9 OR joined report Batt.	40.888
— " —	20th		Sustained shelling short from 1 am to 5 am on Batt H.Q's Hvy casualties in H.Q Coy. Coys are busy about finish hour working on consolidation of front line & installing the new BROEMBEEK with a & new to getting across into Poelcapelle bridgeheads. Enemy fairly quiet — Our own guns very numerous & heavies plastered continually from about 1 WYX corps. At "night" W boy tried BROEMBEEK TO — Failed to pass bridgeheads "y" boy tried to find a crossing & bridges had existed on night of 19th but destroyed been blown in by shell fire — Batt is relieved in the front line by 1st NEWFOUNDLAND Regt & returns to Camps at 13.9 at close to ELVERDINGHE. Total casualties 18 OR killed 55 OR wounded	40. 888 40.815
ABBIMGLY camp B.7.C.66	21.		Batt moved at 2pm to camps as per Margin. Draft 26 OR join report Batt	40.841
— " —	22nd		Organization of Coys. 4 OR evacuated, 1 OR suspected self-inflicted wound.	40.836

Army Form C. 2118.

WAR DIARY
or
INTELLIGENCE SUMMARY.
(Erase heading not required.)

Summary of Events and Information — AUGUST 1917

Place	Date	Hour	Summary of Events and Information	Remarks and references to Appendices
ABBINGLY Camp	23rd		Batt work on Artillery Track 11 repairing same from pipe line to ELVERDINGHE	
"			– WOESTEN Road. 2 OR killed Aterted 86th T.M.B, 1 OR wounded (Point duty) 3 OR Evacuated	40.830
"	24th		Batt continued same work as yesterday. 1 OR returned from Hospital	40.831
"	25. "		Batt moved 2.45 pm to CHARTERHOUSE Camp just in front of (1½ E. on ½) ELVER – DINGHE [BELGIUM 28.N.W.] joining B.Q.C. accommodation Tents & shelters – all in rattled down by 3.30 pm – Brigade moved in support to 87th Bde. Draft 4 OR joined 87 Bat. 2 OR to 86th T.M.Bty. 1 OR to Base unfit	40.832
CHARTERHOUSE 26th Camp B.Q.C.			Divine Service for all denominations. Batt work further up on Track 11. Draft 50 OR joined 87 Bat	40.882
"	27th "		Batt work 2 hours in Morning & 2 in afternoon on Track 11. Draft 8 OR joined 87 Bat 1 OR transferred to R.E. To Hospital Evacuees 12. 5 R	40.877
"	28th "		Batt work morning on Track 11. Move by Tram from ELVERDINGHE at 11 pm to PROVIN – march to PETWORTH Camp PROVEN 3 Area all in settled down by 3 pm accommodation Tents & bivouacs. Transport sent by road – Details from Divisional area report Batt at FLURDINGHE	40. 877

Army Form C. 2118.

WAR DIARY
or
INTELLIGENCE SUMMARY.
(Erase heading not required.)

Instructions regarding War Diaries and Intelligence Summaries are contained in F. S. Regs., Part II. and the Staff Manual respectively. Title pages will be prepared in manuscript.

Place	Date	Hour	Summary of Events and Information	Remarks and references to Appendices
PETWORTH CAMP			1st month of AUGUST 1917 —	
	29th		Return & reinforcements from Corps [29th Inf Batt] join Batt. Bry Sport	
X25d.47 (Petworth 15.5F)			on of grounds. Clearing up & inspection by C.O.	
			Men left for hospital 2 OR. Remained 3 OR. Draft 41 —	40-917.
	30th		Company Training – broke up unselled – draft 86R Joined 2 OR from hospitals	40-927
	31st		Company Training – 2 OR rejoined from hospitals – 2 OR to Base unfit —	40-927
			+ Miscellaneous +	
			Major. A. MOORE D.S.O. commanded the Batt. in the line 6th to 9th inst. in —	
			absence – Lt Col. H. NELSON D.S.O. Liaison Officer with GUARD'S Division	
			Major A. MOORE D.S.O. again in command of Batt in the line night of	
			15th to 20th inst. inclusive – Lt Col. H. NELSON D.S.O. in command of	
			86th Brigade from 16th to 23rd inst.; Brig genl R.J. SELF unable to carry on owing	
			to illness – Brig. Genl G.R.H. CHEAP. M.C. taken command 86th Bde	
			24th inst. Lt Col. H. NELSON D.S.O. in temporary command of 88th Bde	
			27th inst in absence of Brig Genl CAYLEY on leave –	

Vol 18. 86/29

17X
9 sheets

WAR DIARY
of
1st Royal Malta Engineers

In Month of September 1917

Volume 30

Army Form C. 2118.

WAR DIARY
or
INTELLIGENCE SUMMARY.
(Erase heading not required.)

Place	Date	Hour	Summary of Events and Information	Remarks and references to Appendices.
PETWORTH CAMP X.25.A.4.7 [Belgium 19 SE]	1st		Company Training - Bathe for spots in afternoon. 2.OR from hospital. Draft 3.OR joined, 1 to BASE infil 2 OR to hospital 1OR.	40.929
	2nd		Divine Service for all denominations. Company football competition W. v. Z. Y v X - 1st named won - 2nd Lt W.F SPIESS joined reported X Coy.	40.929
"	3rd		Company Training - Company football competition - W. beat Y final Coy football competition. 2nd Lt J.B JOHNSTON joined posted "Y" Coy, 1 OR struck off on Draft. 2 OR Base infil, 1OR to hospital. 1OR from hospital & Draft 1BCR joined.	40.942
"	4th		Bn. ceremonial Parade in morning for presentation of Honours by G.O.C Division [9th DeLISLE]. The Bn. awarded the following for gallantry in action during period 6th to 20th August 17. Some drunk from prostration through Wounds & other causes 2 M.C., 3 D.C.M., 12 M.Ms. MILITARY CROSS - 2/Lt R MAGUIRE, D.P.WAGNER; DISTINGUISHED CONDUCT MEDAL - 13750. R.S. Major H MURPHY, C.Q.M.S. 2701 L.BYRNE [wounded], 11167 Sgt P WAINE; MILITARY MEDAL - 10605 Sgt J.OCKENDON 23002 Cpl T.MORRISSEY, 10347 Sgt R PRESTAGE, 4907 Sgt P BROPHY - already awarded DCM [Hospital], 20825 L/Cpl J LYNN [wounded], 18472 L/cpl FINNERTY [wounded], 10026 Pte J TERRET, 7889 Pte S.LETT, 25184 Pte TOWNSEND [wounded], 25243 Pte W.LAWLESS, 2.8739 M.M.GREEN, 4100 4 Pte J.WATSON [wounded]. Weather Very fine. The display by the Bn. Before Very good. In the afternoon inter-company Run	

WAR DIARY
or
INTELLIGENCE SUMMARY.
(Erase heading not required.)

Army Form C. 2118.

Place	Date	Hour	Summary of Events and Information	Remarks and references to Appendices
PETWORTH CAMP	Sept 4th		continued from by W Coy	September 1917
"	5th		Company training hard in morning. In afternoon Batt beat 497th (Kent) Field Coy R.E in the Bde football competition 3-0, but it was a bit rough well improve next match.	40-942
"	6th		2nd/Lts. C.T. WINGFIELD & F.F. SMITH join posted to "Z" Coy, 1 O.R Evacuated.	42.942
"			Company training. In the afternoon Batt boxing competition most events won by representatives of W.Coy. Some good fights. 1 O.R returns from hospital	42-942
"	7th		morning spent in gas gym. "Smartest Platoon competition" in the Batt, best platoon of the Batt to compete against best Platoon of the other Batts in Bde.	
			afternoon Batt Sports. Some good performances. Lieut Gen Briggs visited camp 86th Bde staff present also representatives of Division & the units & Blown Re brigaden. Staff nurses & R.A.M.C staff of neighbouring C.C.S's. "X" Coy won the Cup. Presented by Capt L.H McFEELY M.C. (In 2 coys) for the Coy getting most points in the Sports. Draft 40.R joined.	
			3 O.R. Evacuated. 1 O.R returned from hospital.	42.981
	8th		Judging Matters continued in morning - afternoon boxing competition be - tween units of Bde at Bde H.Q. Fine raised rings etc raised there.	

WAR DIARY
or
INTELLIGENCE SUMMARY.
(Erase heading not required.)

Army Form C. 2118.

for month of September 1917

Place	Date	Hour	Summary of Events and Information	Remarks and references to Appendices
PETWORTH Camp	8th		Continued. Batt. did very well. Heavy 2 men in Several finals of Heavy weight 2 in Middle, 1 in Welter, 2 in Light. Finals tomorrow afternoon	
			1 OR Transferred to R.E., 1 R.S. Base Depot	42-977
"	9th		Divine service for all denominations. In afternoon 2.30pm Bde Cross Country Race. 89th Bde entered 1st 34 points, Batt. 2nd 31points, 1st Lancs Fus. 3rd 23 points. At 5.30pm finals of Boxing. Batt. did splendidly. Runners up — Heavy weight wt 10.24 Sgt MURPHY; Middle 8.10 Sgt McGUILL B, Light 7334 Sgt BURKE P. The Batt. won the Cups very kindly presented by Lt Col. Bate Major [Capt. T.J. DERDEN D.S.O.M.C] for the Batt. doing best in the Boxing. "Y" Company at West a Platoon from "Y" Coy came 1st in Batt. Competition in Inter Platoon at West 1st Coy 2nd, 2nd by 3rd, 3rd X Coy 4th = 42.977	
"	10th		Batt. move to camp in front of ELVERDINGHE [18NW/ B9.a.8.8.] by tram from PROVEN. arrived new camp about 8.30 a.m. — working parties under R.E. began at 12 noon. Two further parties at night — Parties total 450. Camp uncomfortable 2/Lt. A.J. WALKER to Hospital 9 inst — 2/Lt. J.L. DEVOY returned from Hpt. 11 inst. 1 OR returned from Hpt. Batt. 11. OR joined, evacuated 4. OR 7/11 B.B. MURPHY to Hospital with whitlow wound	41-987

Army Form C. 2118.

WAR DIARY
or
INTELLIGENCE SUMMARY.
(Erase heading not required.)

Instructions regarding War Diaries and Intelligence Summaries are contained in F. S. Regs., Part II. and the Staff Manual respectively. Title pages will be prepared in manuscript.

for Month of September 1917 —

Place	Date	Hour	Summary of Events and Information	Remarks and references to Appendices
OXFORD Camp near ELVERDINGHE SH.W/B.9.d.88	11=		Working parties as before. Inspecting road IRON CROSS - VULCAN CROSSING. Moving dumps forward etc. Working parties have 3 wounded, camp shelled at night. 1 man killed.	
			Bicycle Sports at PETWORTH Camp - Batt won most events - Batt won most events. Platoon Championships. Special prizes presented by Brigadier General. 2/Lt G.B.HOLLOM twice open high jump, officers relay race. also won by us. No.10021 Pte P.O'CONNOR wins most events for the Batt. Beautiful day. Many Visitors at the Sports which were most successful.	41-987
— " —	12=		Batt found same working parties. Bde football competition. Batt beaten by 2nd Ry. Fusiliers 4 - 2 — 1 OR rejoined from Bde H.Qrs. 1 OR from desertion.	41-989
— " —	13=		Working parties as before, no further casualties. Parties have difficulty in proceeding as work have delayed by heavy enemy barrage on PILKEM RIDGE. 1 OR killed in action 11th inst. 3 OR wounded 9 & OR missing 11th inst.	41-984
— " —	14=		Batt return by train to PROVEN arriving PETWORTH Camp about 12-45 p.m. 4 OR evacuated	41-980
PETWORTH Camp. PROVEN 3 miles X.25.d.4.7 Belgium 19.S.E	15=		Company Training. 2 OR evacuated. 2/Lt B.BLAYLOCK struck off strength taken on in War by 29th Depot Batt.	40-978

Army Form C. 2118.

WAR DIARY
or
INTELLIGENCE SUMMARY.
(Erase heading not required.)

Instructions regarding War Diaries and Intelligence Summaries are contained in F. S. Regs., Part II. and the Staff Manual respectively. Title pages will be prepared in manuscript.

Summary of Events and Information for month of September 1917.

Place	Date	Hour	Summary of Events and Information	Remarks and references to Appendices
PETWORTH Camp	16th		Divine Service in all denominations. Batt. left camp for HERZEELE training area about 3.30 pm arrived 6.30 pm Staff. 6 OR. join H.QR. Somewhere.	40.980
HERZEELE	17th		Batt. training 8 am to 1 pm	40.980
—	18th		Batt. training in syllabus. Schemes for Coy Com. on afternoon on Bde field day for (19th inst) the next day during afternoon. Preliminary rounds of Divisional Boxing Competition take place at Bde Hqrs (ie 86 Bde H2) near PETWORTH Camp. Batt. doing well. Runff. 9. OR arrive 25th Depot Batt.	40.989
—	19th		Bde in attack - practice - 1st R.W.B.Fus on Right 1st Lanc.Fus on left. take BLUE line (1st objective) 2nd Royal Fus on right 16th Mids Regt on left. take RED line (2nd objective) - G.O.C. Division pleased with manner attack was carried out. Batt. move back to PETWORTH Camp at 2.15 pm.
Semi finals & finals of Divisional Boxing at 86th: 13 Bde HQrs. 86th Bde won the Championships. the Batt. contributing largely to this by winning the Heavies (43075 L/Cpl MOLLOY.M) Lightweight (7334 Sgt BURKE.P.), 40449 Pte MURPHY.D. beaten in final of feathers, 10424 Sgt MURPHY.P. beaten Semi final of Middles. 8170 Z/Sgt McGUILL.B. our best boxer, unable to box in Middles having hurt his knee. Gen. DELISLE G.O.C. Div. presented the Prizes.	40.989

A 6945 Wt. W11422 M1180 350,000 12/16 D.D. & L. Forms/C/2118/14.

WAR DIARY
or
INTELLIGENCE SUMMARY.
(Erase heading not required.)

Army Form C. 2118.

Summary for month of September 1917.

Place	Date	Hour	Summary of Events and Information	Remarks and references to Appendices
PETWORTH Camp	20th		Company training - Half 10% Details under Capt. W.R. OULTON. M.C. move in the Morning by train to 29th Depot Batt. BOLLEZEELE - 10R. wounded	40.988
"	21st		Batt. move to ETON Camp near ELVERDINGHE, entraining PROVEN at 1.15 pm; take over Camp from 1st WELSH GUARDS - Remaining half of 10% move to HOUNSLOW Camp [28 N.W/A11.C] where all 86th Bde. Details are concentrated - 2nd I.D. MACKENZIE is ammunition is leaving to join 2nd place in Company. Competition open to all Officers of the 86th Bde. C.Q.M.S. - L. Byrne (8901) awarded CROIX de GUERRE (he is already in possession of the D.C.M. & M.M.)	
ETON Camp [28 N.W B7d]	22nd		Batt. found 2 working Parties one at 12.15 am + the other at 6.15 am, parties of 40 + 50 respectively to work under R.E. 2/Lt C.T. WINGFIELD to 86th T.M. By. for permanent attachment, also 10R to that unit. 2 OR Evacuated - Enemy Aeroplane fired nature.	40.986
"	23rd		Divine Service for all denominations. Batt. work on TRACK Eleven. Weather continues fine	39.985
"	24th		Batt. work on TRACK 11. 10R. ammunition (22/9/17) 2 OR wounded, 1 same 10 OR from at Depot	39.985 39.992
"	25th		Batt work 3 hours in morning on TRACK 11. Beautiful day. E.A's bomb near Camp 36 Mules killed - 12 men killed & 3 wounded belonging to R.F.A. 1 OR struck by shrapnel so severe as Lewis not far from this Camp	39.794

WAR DIARY
INTELLIGENCE SUMMARY
(Erase heading not required.)

Army Form C. 2118.

Place	Date	Hour	Summary of Events and Information	Remarks and references to Appendices
ETON Camp	26th		September 1917 – Company training. Baths for the men – Divisional Band plays a selection of music in camp at 5.30 p.m. – Some new draughts. 2 O.R.	
			Generation Joined – Lieut W.E. CALBECK & 2/Lieut M. LAYTON from Depot Batt. 25 inst.	41-989
— —	27th		Company training – C.O. visits lines. It to be taken over on 1st Instance.	
			After [illegible] R. McGUIRE 3/Lt. C. LONERGEY evacuated for disposal to England. 1 O.R. wounded Kent. MELVIN E wounded 1 O.R. Base M.G.C.	40.987
— —	28th		Y & Z Coys leave camp 5 p.m. to relieve 12th KINGS LIVERPOOL Regt in front line details – Somme [illegible] left half (Q.3.S.) in support line – but Hd. Qtrs BLACK HORSE LANE MERCKEM Rd C.17.15 – Z Coy on left. Y Coy on Right. – Z Coy have casualties going up – Relief complete at 11.30 p.m. Line held by Posts – Officer patrols all night. Enemy very quiet.	
			On the alert – Night on the whole quiet – Draft 7 O.R. Joined Dept. Batt.	40-994
LANGEMARK & U.23.C.1-7.5.	29th		Any fairly quiet. Relieved by 16th MIDDLESEX Regt. Relief completed by midnight. Shelling on Eilow trestle very heavy on the companies. Also many gas shells but men very tired Coy. Fig also meets return to ETon Camp difficult – all in by 3.30 am Casualties 1 O.R. killed	

WAR DIARY
or
INTELLIGENCE SUMMARY.
(Erase heading not required.)

Army Form C. 2118.

Summary of Events and Information September 1917.

Place	Date	Hour	Summary of Events and Information	Remarks and references to Appendices
	29th	continued	for month of — 13 OR wounded. Lieut. LAKINS joined Depot Batt 28th inst. 2/Lt. A.G. SIDWELL also arrived from hospital	41-930
ETON Camp	30th		Batt. spent day resting — Col. A. NELSON D.S.O proceeded to take over command of the 88th Bde of this Division (29th) vice Brig Genl. DE CAYLEY C.M.G wounded (gas) — Great regret in the Batt at losing Col NELSON under whose able command the Batt has always maintained a high state of efficiency — Major A. MOORE D.S.O. assumed command of the Batt.	41-930

1/R Dubs

Capt Tarleton
October 1917

NOT FOR
VISITORS

Captain G.W.B. Tarleton

1.

On the night of the 3rd/4th October, 1917, the 1/Royal Dublin Fusiliers relieved the 16th Middx. Regt. in the right sector of the Divisional Front. The two leading Companies for the assault "Y" Coy on the right and "Z" Coy on the left moved straight into EAGLE TRENCH and put out covering posts. The section Trench Mortar Battery formed up behind "Y" Coy and behind them again was the flanking detachment 16/Middlesex Regt. "W" Coy who were to be in support during the assault were lined up in shell holes to the left rear of the Trench Mortar Battery section and "X" Coy in reserve were behind "W" in shell holes.

The objectives of Companies were as follows:- "Z" Coy to capture post at 45 K. on the STADEN Railway and GOED TER VESTEN FARM and dig on a line approximately U.17.d.0.3. to U.18.d.0.5. "Y" Coy on the right to capture CHINESES HOUSE and the four Blockhouses at U.18.c.4.6. and to reach the line U.18.c.6.7. to U.18.d.3.8. digging on the line from the latter point to join up with "Z" Coy at U.18.d.0.5. "W" Coy were to move behind the leading Coy and consolidate a line approximately from U.17.d.7.0. to U.18.c.4.0. "X" Coy to moved into EAGLE TRENCH immediately the leading Companies three had got clear of it. Flanking Detachment 16/Middlesex Regt. were to cover the right flank during the advance and upon "Y" Coy reaching their objective to dig in at approximately at U.18.d.1.5. ready to beat off any counter-attack threatening from that direction.

The joining up of the Battalion was carried out very quietly and effectively. The night was dark and no movement could be seen by the enemy. There was very little shelling through the night and though the enemy shelled slightly more heavily about 5.0 a.m. as is his daily custom in that region the Companies had very few casualties. Immediately upon relief of 16/Middlesex Regt. Companies proceeded to draw their battle stores from the dumps in the vicinity - sandbags, flares, S.O.S. Rockets alone were taken up by the Companies together with one day's ration and iron ration. Tools and Lewis Guns were brought up in advance of the Battalion and dumped near GREEN HILL where Companies picked them up on their way from camp to the line. The chief stores drawn from the dumps were bombs and S.A.A. and in addition Companies had in their possession large quantities of tape.

By zero less one hour all Companies were in their correct positions. Some hot tea in petrol tins which were wrapped round in hay and p-ut into packs had been brought up by mules, with compies as far as the junction of Hunter Switch and the Mule Track and this was greatly appreciated by the men with a half tot of rum.

The barrage appeared to open half a minute too soon on the right but came down punctually on our front to the time. All ranks praise the accuracy and volume of the barrage though several admit that they were wounded by getting too close under it. It is interesting to note here that it was extremely difficult at that hour to ascertain the line of the barrage after the first lift.

Immediately the barrage came down the two leading companies who had left their positions and strengthened them gradually as zero approached dashed out and got as close to barrage as possible moving in lines of sections. The remaining bodies all came forward and maintained the same formation.

"W" Coy were the first to report their objective taken and notified Battalion Headquarters that "Y" Coy were making good progress. A part of "W" Coy however overstepped the objective and moved up behind   Coy eventually taking up a position about the four Blockhouses   18.c.4.6. "Z" Coy captured T. GOED TER VESTEN FARM and took sixty- prisoners and also captured K.45 with two machine guns and prisoners. Twenty other prisoners were captured in shell holes between these two points. At K.45 however "Z" Coy's post was heavy machine gun fire from across the Broembeek and as the enemy   been very much
consolidated in a shell hole 12 yards south of it. This gave their new post the advantage of having the old enemy wire in front of them as an obstacle.

No information could be obtained from "Y" Coy all of whose officers had become casualties and whose Company Sergeant Major was killed. By a Personal reconnaissance however carried out by the Intelligence Officer they were seen to be on their objective and consolidating being in touch with the Seaforth Highlanders of the 4th Division on the right. About 1.30 p.m. a small local counter-attack came from the direction of KORTEBEEK FARM and the Seaforth Highlanders seeing the gap between certain portions of "Y" Coy's flank and the enemy dubbling forward to it commenced to go back taking with them that part of "Y" Coy nearest themselves. The counter-attack however was easily beaten off and the Seaforths returning swung too much over to the right taking with them the party of "Y" Coy of whom no news has since been heard.

About 5.0 p.m. however the Warwickshire Regt. coming up to support the Seaforth Highlanders noticing the gap caused in our line by the centre which had remained firm and details on the right which had swung over too much to that flank sent over one Coy to occupy the gap. Throughout the afternoon the Companies were subjected to fairly heavy shelling but they had dug themselves in well and did not have excessive casualties. At dusk that evening two platoons of 1st K.O.S.B's came in to EAGLE TRENCH to reinforce our Reserve Coy now only two platoons strong one platoon having been sent up to reinforce the Centre Coy consolidating the line approximately U.17.c.8.4. - U.18.d.2.4. and digging a support line approximately at U.18.d.0.1.

About 9.30 p.m. one Coy 2/Royal Fusiliers relieved "X" Coy in EAGLE TRENCH and this Coy was sent forward to reinforce the very thin line of "Y" Coy consolidating a line from the four blockhouses along the Green Line to point 38.

This line was dug in rear of the Warwicks as it was considered likely that the latter Regiment being out of their area might be ordered to withdraw at any moment thus leaving the most important position uncovered and leaving a way open for an enemy counter-attack which would come at this point if anywhere and would very dangerously expose 19 Metre Hill the key of the position.

The night of the 4th was calm - the next morning opened very clear and there was considerable aerial activity. The country however was in a very wet condition owing to the continuous drizzle of rain on the day of the 4th and the somewhat heavier showers during the night. About 1 p.m. the enemy shelling became heavy and there was continuous rifle and machine gun sniping by the enemy from the BROEMBEEK. "X" Coy however succeeded in pushing posts well out to within 50 yards of the BROEMBEEK to maintain better observations of the enemy movements.

During the night of the 5th there was heavy enemy shelling and owing to the relieving Battalion not knowing the locality and guides straying the relief was not complete till 2.0 a.m. and the Battalion returned to ETON CAMP.

Total casualties for the tour were:-

	Officers.	Men.
Missing	2	25
Wounded	7	103
Killed	-	21

One officer of those wounded is remaining with Unit.

Communication was difficult through the day of the assault telephone wires to Brigade Headquarters were continually being cut and remained useless for long periods. Signalling by lamp was fairly successful but is dependant on weather conditions. Telephone lines to the forward troops could not be maintained and were at once severed when repaired. A forward Signals Station together with a relay runner post and Battalion forward Headquarters were established in EAGLE TRENCH, but as the region between EAGLE TRENCH and Battalion Headquarters in LANGEMARCK was more heavily shelled than any other area. The Signal Station in EAGLE TRENCH was of little use though it provided a good relay runner post. Communications by runner was the most satisfactory although casualties hampered this. Pigeons were not satisfactory as the hours during which they can be used are necessarily limited on days when there is a mist and they are also apparently useless at night. Communication is the greatest problem. Wirless messages were not picked up.

The medical arrangements were satisfactory. The Regimental Air post was in EAGLE TRENCH and all cases from the leading Companies were brought there and sent on to the "PIG & WHISTLE." Any delay that was caused was due to the extraordinary heavy casualties amongst R.A.M.C. personnel who had to pass through LANGEMARCK on their journeys and this place was continually shelled. The Liaison with the flanks was not very satisfactory but as the Headquarters of the Battalions in the assault on the right being close to our own forward Battalion Headquarters there was no great apprehension as regards the situation. The flanking detachment 16/Middlesex Regiment suffered heavily in casualties and no message of any sort was received from them throughout the 4th/5th. They probably found themselves among elements of the 4th Division in the same manner as certain details of our "Y" Coy did. The supply of ammunition, grenades, etc., were satisfactory. Companies used the two dumps in EAGLE TRENCH during and after the assault and every effort was made to fill up these dumps from those at Battalion Headquarters and at REITRES FARM. The latter place however receives more than ordinary attention from the enemy artillery. During the assault the men carried the following:-

Bombers	4 bombs.
Rifle Grenadiers	4 Rifle Grenades.
Riflemen	170 rounds.
Lewis Guns	32 magazines per gun.

4 sandbags per man. 50% shovels.

The leading waves of the leading Companies were however more lightly dressed than the rear waves. One point which has not been stated however was the communication with the Artillery. There was a liaison officer with Battalion Headquarters and all requests made to the artillery at various points were at once carried out.

In conclusion it is interesting to note that the enemy was completely taken by surprise when our attack was launched. This is borne out by the fact that many of them were captured with their boots off (they nearly all had two pairs in their possession) also their shelters had blankets and waterproof sheets and some were caught inside these. There was a great quantity of beer, cigars and rum in dugouts and shelters and shell holes were organised by erecting uprights and covering them for half the diameter with boarding-rabbit wire and earth on top.

                        (Sgd) G. W. B. TARLETON.

                              Captain & Adjutant,

7/10/17.   1st Bn. Royal Dublin Fusiliers.

for M F O'Donnell
, B Dubos

NOT FOR
VISITORS

1st. Royal Dublin Fusiliers

A Brief War Record of Lt. M. F. O'Donnell,
M.C., 12, Leinster Sq., Rathmines, Dublin.

Joined Pals' Battalion (7th Royal Dublin Fusiliers), 28th November, 1914. Saw service in the ranks at Gallipoli, Servia, and Salonika. Was mentioned in General Milne's Salonika Despatches (December 1916). Left Salonika 1st December 1916 to proceed home for a course in a Cadet School. Joined 7th Officers' Cadet Battalion at Moore Park, Fermoy, on 3rd January 1917. Was gazetted Second Lieutenant to the 11th Battalion Royal Dublin Fusiliers on 20th April 1917. Joined 8th Battn. Roy. Dub. Fus., in France on 14th June 1917. Was wounded in action at Ypres on 1st Augt. 1917, but remained with Battalion until 4th August. Went to Hospital 4th August, rejoined Battalion 13th August. Remained with Battalion until amalgamation of 8/9th and after disbandment became attached to the 2nd Battalion Roy. Dub. Fus. Proceeded home on leave 20th March 1918. Was ordered off boat at Le Havre 22nd March (All leave stopped owing to the Bosch offensive). Became attached to 1st Roy. Dub. Fus. 20th April 1918. Remained with Battalion until severely wounded 21st October 1918 . Awarded M.C. 4th September 1918 - Ploegsteert. Awarded 1st bar to M.C. 14th October 1918 - Ledgehem. Awarded 2nd bar to M.C. 20th October 1918 - near St. Louis (Courtrai). Invalided out of the Army owing to wounds 29th July 1919. Rank Lieutenant.

1st Battalion The Royal Dublin Fusiliers.

MEMORANDA.

from M. F. O'Donnell, 12 Leinster Square, Rathmines,
Dublin.

2/Lt. Michael F. O'Donnell became attached to the 1st Battalion The Royal Dublin Fusiliers on or about the 21st April 1918. The Battalion was then resting in a small village called (I think) Beausingham - about three kilometres outside Aires. The Battalion was commanded by Lt.Col. Moore, D.S.O., and Captain C.W. Bailey was Adjutant. Lt. M.F. O'Donnell was accompanied by 2/Lt. M.J. McNulty, and both were posted to "Y" Company. Our leave had been stopped, and were ordered off the leave boat at Le Havre on the morning of the 22nd March to await orders to rejoin our Unit. Capt. Jackson who had been formerly Adjutant of the 8th Royal Dublin Fusiliers was Company Commander of "Y" Company. The 1st Battalion Roy. Dub. Fus., had at this time the remnants of the 2nd Battalion and the disbanded 8/9th after the March Offensive, and the rank and file were supernumerary to Establishment. In consequence, about 125 men of the Royal Dublin Fusiliers were transferred to the Royal Irish Regiment who had suffered heavily during the March offensive, and 2/Lt. M.F. O'Donnell was detailed to conduct the men to that Regiment. This he did, and obtained receipt from the Adjutant of the 2nd Royal Irish Regt.

The 1st Roy. Dub. Fus. had been awaiting orders to rejoin their old division - the 29th - the 16th had ceased to exist as far as a fighting division was concerned. The order soon came along and the Battalion moved off and with the 1st Lancashire Fusiliers and 2nd Royal Fusiliers became the 86th Brigade of that famous division. We were received with open arms, and the Brigadier-General, and Divisional General spoke of the glorious deeds of the 1st Battalion, and were glad to have the Battalion chasing the Hun who had now been brought to a standstill.

On the 1st May, 2/Lt. O'Donnell was detailed to take over from a Company of the 2nd Irish Guards who had become attached to the 32nd Division. Their Company Headquarters were situate at Le Tir Anglais - near the village of La Motte on the outskirts of Nieppe Forest. The Coy. Commander had been suffering from the effects of gas, and the Guards had many casualties from this inhuman method of warfare. He was a subaltern, and I think had only another second-lieutenant in the Company. He stuck to his Company however, and refused to leave it until they left for a much needed rest. Father Browne, D.S.O. was Chaplain to the Guards and we had a chat over various matters - particularly regarding the death of the heroic Rev. W. Doyle, M.C. who gave his life at Freizenburgh on or about the 17th August 1917. Father Doyle was attached the 48th Brigade 16th Division (Irish), and spent a good deal, if not all his time, practically with the Battalions - the 8th Battn. chiefly in which I had been a Subaltern.

I shall never forget the discipline and clock-work precision of that Guard's Company when the men fell in at Le Tir Anglais before leaving that sector. One would think they were on a barrack square when they were ordered to "Slope

Arms" - one - two - three. They still carried with them discipline unsurpassed - although they had a most gruelling time.

We had several working parties, under the supervision of the Royal Engineers in Nieppe Forest - Breastworks etc. were constructed, which were known as La Motte Defences. The Lancashire Fusiliers had been in the line at this time, the Royal Fus. in support (I think this was the order) and the Royal Dublins in reserve. We suffered mostly from Gas Shells, and when we moved into the line - which was really an outpost line in front of the Forest, we had been given instructions to make as little movement as possible. This warning was, to my mind, unnecessary - as the trench we occupied was only about three feet deep and were told not to deepen or widen it - as new soil would give our position away to the enemy. The weather, fortunately, was very good at this time, and the Bosch was holding Vieux Berquin, and some farm houses about two hundred yards in front of our outposts. We got only one meal perdiem during our tour in the line. This was brought to us at about 2.30 in the morning. The Battalion, in the month of June was detailed to the Petit Sec Bois Sector where I left, (on leave). Meanwhile a raid was carried out by "Y" Company under Captain Alexander, D.C.M., who with two subalterns Ross and McGowan were very successful - made good some ground - took several prisoners - and established their former reputation held by the Battalion. Alexander and McGowan were each awarded an M.C., and the rank and file were also awarded decorations. July found the Division resting at Campeigne. Divisional training for the coming advance was the order of the day and "Y" Company was taken over by Capt. Bryan Desmond Hughes, M.C., who had been formerly in the 8th and 8/9th Royal Dublin Fusiliers. He had come from the Reserve Battalion at (I think) Grimsby. We had been great friends and were glad to be together again in the good cause. But a five weeks' course had been ordered me by the Adjutant, and I found myself at Wisques^x - near St. Omer - going through all the

---

x Won medal officers' welter weight boxing competition at Wisques.
: : officers' -do- Recreational training Competition at Wisques.

---

peregrinations of "forming fours" &c. with a good many worn-out officers after the March offensive. I am sorry, however, to relate that the death of my esteemed Company Commander reached me at Wisques, during a raid on the Strazeele sector, and we lost another valuable N.C.O. Sergt.Major Kavanagh, Medaille Militaire, and a few others in this raid. Colonel Moore, our Battalion Commander, came to Wisques while I was in the 2nd Army School there on a Battalion Commander's Course, and he told me all the news concerning the Battalion. I again reached the Battalion Headquarters at Hazebrouck on or about 22nd August 1918. Major Heffernan, D.S.O., M.C., was second-in-command of the Battalion. Some of the subalterns who had a rough time in the line were resting there. At this time the order was to take only a certain percentage of officers into the line. The first evening of my arrival at Hazebrouck 2/Lt. O'Donnell "got down to it" about 12.5 a.m. He had been in bed about half an hour when the Quarter Master came to his billets with a message from the Adjutant that Captain Alexander was badly gassed and that I was to

report to Battalion Headquarters and take over his platoon.
Lt. Cassidy, M.C. had taken over command of the company.
A horse was provided for me, and we rode to Strazeele - a
guide accompanying me who by the way did not know where
Battalion Headquarters were. Gas shells tormented us on our
journey to Strazeele, and on reaching Strazeele 2/Lt.
O'Donnell dismissed the guide, and was left to wander round
all the tumbled down houses at Strazeele to find the Adjutant.
Capt. Maguire, M.C. was Adjutant of the Battalion whom I
found at about 2.15 a.m. resting, very much tired after a
strenuous day. He provided a guide for me to report to Lt.
Cassidy whom we found before day-break with another subaltern
2/Lt. Lennon - both very badly shaken from the Bosch shelling.
Nothing of much importance occurred in this sector, except a
few raids carried out by the Battalion but a good deal of
wiring etc. was done by the Battalion. The Australians were
on our left. They were glad to be beside the Dublins.
Some of the Australian officers told us so, and naturally we
reciprocated the good wishes.

Our Adjutant left the Battalion, through illness, and he
never rejoined the Battalion up to the time I was wounded
severely on the 21st October 1918.

Colonel Moore, D.S.O. did me the honour on or about the
26th August of offering me the post of Assistant Adjutant to
the Battalion. This I politely refused, and he did not
force the duty upon me; although he expressed the wish that I
should do so. I told him I preferred being with my Coy.
and a substitute was found in Lt. L----- Strange, but none the
less true, our Company was detailed for a raid two days'
afterwards. Lt. Lennon and I volunteered. We each had
twenty-five men, and were detailed to scupper three farm
houses in front of our line which were, according to an
Officer's patrol report the day before, held by a Bosch
Officer and about thirty-five men. We moved into the jumping-
off position without any mishap, and waited until the box-
barrage went down. On we went to our allotted task got into
and around the three farm-houses - Lennon on the right,
O'Donnell on the left - only to find that the Bosch had vacated
the buildings. We discovered only one dead Bosch whose
shoulder straps we cut. Lt. Lennon and one or two of his
men apparently got too close to our barrage and were wounded.

On the 2nd September 1918 we got orders to move to La
Romarin and on the evening of the 3rd our orders were to take
Ploegsteert at all costs. We had to go through the 32nd
Division who then held Le Romarin. The order of attack was
Dublins on the right, Lancashire Fusiliers on the left, Royals
in support. Two Companies of the Dublins W and X led, "Y"
Company formed a defensive flank to the "W" Coy. on the right,
and "Z" Coy. was in reserve. We moved off before dawn, and had
not proceeded far when we were trench-mortared by the Bosch.
Our right was in the air - as no other troops appeared when
dawn broke. On we pushed - suffering severely but never
wavering until we got to a dyke about 900 yards from Ploegsteert. This occurred at 8.30 a.m. where we were eventually
held up. The enemy shelling was very severe, and machine-
gun fire was played mercilessly on us. Lt. M.J. McNulty was
in command of the leading platoon of "Y" company forming the
defensive flank to "W" Coy. under Capt. S.G. Darling, M.C.
2/Lt. O'Donnell was in command of the 2nd platoon forming the
defensive flank, while 2/Lt. Chudleigh commanded the third
platoon and the fourth platoon was under a N.C.O. The leading
Company had suffered severely prior to being held up, and the

going at this point seemed rather sticky. O'Donnell went forward to the leading Company Commander who was sending back a message for reinforcements. When he discovered McNulty[x] out

---

[x] The least I can say of McNulty is that if ever officer or man deserved a V.C. McNulty did. (M.F. O'D).

---

in front - after capturing two Bosch machine guns - a heavy and a light machine gun. The Company Commander asked me to go to McNulty's assistance. McNulty and his men were about forty yards in front. Our conversation took place in the farmyard of a good-sized house on the main road to Ploegsteert. The road divided the Companies in attack. McNulty, as soon as he saw me, shouted "Mick, are there any stretcher bearers there" - and on running towards him with my runner, McNulty had fallen - wounded in the throat from a machine gun bullet. He had previously lost a portion of his thumb and one or two fingers and was bleeding profusely. The poor fellow's life was fast ebbing. On kneeling over him to ask if he had any request to make or message to send home - my runner, Private Coffey - was wounded in the wrist beside me. Poor McNulty never spoke. He had only five men left in his Platoon. The rest were casualties. I took over the remnants of his platoon, and we took cover in the drain which was about five feet deep and contained about 18 inches of water. We got touch with Capt. Noblett in command of "X" Company on the left who told me of his casualties. Here we reorganised and formed a line with the drain and awaited orders. Messages had been sent back from time to time reporting position and casualties. At 3 p.m. in the afternoon, a message was received that a barrage would be sent down and that we were to advance under this creeping barrage until Ploegsteert was taken. Meanwhile the 32nd division were to be seen on our right but at least 500 yards behind the leading Company of the Dublins. I do not think the Lancashires made much progress on our left. They were held up. Under the barrage the Dublins advanced - never faltering - never waivering. The Bosch had very thick wire erected in front of his positions - Machine guns seemed to spring up everywhere - chiefly on our right flank. We hacked our way through the wire, got in among the enemy who failed to meet us, and surrendered rather too willingly. Several of the Bosch bolted for their own lines and were nice targets for our men - firing as we advanced. We reached Ploegsteert, consolidated and were relieved that night by the Royal Fusiliers.[x] We had captured four new field guns - some gave the

---

[x] A/Capt. Noblett was not relieved that night owing to some mistake made by a Company Commander of The Royal Fusiliers. His Company remained in the line until relieved 24 hours afterwards.

---

total number as six, several trench mortars and a great many machine guns. Our casualties were heavy. Roughly four officers (one killed) and about 250 rank and file. Bosch prisoners wearing red brassards carried revolvers. Prisoners numbered about 185 including officers.

We were greatly complimented for this show - by the Brigadier, Divisional Commander, Corps Commander, and General Plumer took the salute from the Battalion as it wended its way from Bailleul through Metern and Merris to Hazebrouck.

Four M.C.s. two D.C.Ms. and 41 Military Medals were allotted to the Battalion for this show.

From Hazebrouck the Battalion went to the Brandhoek area outside Popperinghe, and again went into action on 29th September at Ypres. During this show I was acting Transport Officer. The R.T.O. was on leave. The Battalion got as far as Cheuvelt when it was withdrawn for a rest. The Battalion did very well in this show and received more decorations for bravery etc. We rested at Ypres during the 1st two days of October 1918 whence we were sent to take over from the Royal Scots at Ledgehem. One company of the 1st Battalion (I think) took over from a Company of the 36th Ulster Division on the right at Dadazeele. We spent six days here - until the 8th October and were again withdrawn to Ypres. We had only a few casualties. On the 13th October 1918 we moved from Ypres by the light railway to the jumping off position at Ledgehem Railway Station. "W" Coy. under command of Capt. S.G. Daling, M.C., "X" Coy. under Lt. Blake, "Y" under command of 2/Lt. M.F. O'Donnell, M.C. and "Z" Coy. under Capt. McFeely, D.S.O., M.C., who, by the way, was acting Brigade Major, and rejoined the Battalion to take his old Company into action. The order of attack was "Z" Coy. on the left, "Y" Coy. on the right, "X" and "W" Coys. respectively behind "Z" and "Y". The Leinsters were on the right. We advanced at zero hour under a heavy smoke barrage, and took our objective which was about 2,500 yards east of Ledgehem. Colonel Moore was killed about three hundred yards from the objective. The Battalion then came under the command of Major Rigg. The Lancashire Fusiliers went through us after getting our objective. A Battalion of Newfoundlanders were on the left of our Battalion front. We captured several prisoners and machine guns in this show. The smoke barrage did not clear until about mid-day, and the objective was taken shortly afterwards.

We rested from the 14th to 18th October, and carried out morning parades barefooted in the fields. This order came from Brigade. I turned out with my Platoon Commanders for this parade at 7.30 a.m., and the men appeared to enjoy the parade.

The 19th October found us on the line of March following up the Bosch. He was retiring swiftly, and we were to give him no rest. The 36th Division were on our right while the famous 9th (Scottish) Division were on our left. We went through the (I think) 49th Brigade who had a fairly rough time, and were held up about two kilometres east of Courtrai. We crossed the Lys at Courtrai by means of a temporary bridge erected by the Engineers. One man at a time at intervals of about fifteen paces. The battalion got across without any mishap, and soon found itself in action towards three o'clock in the afternoon of the 20th October. We were informed by our Brigadier that we would meet with machine gun opposition on our right - as from that quarter came most of the opposition. This information turned out correct. The order of attack by the Battalion was "W" Coy. on the right under Capt. Darling, M.C. "X" Coy. under command of Lt. Blake on the left, "Z" Coy. under command of Capt. McFeely, D.S.O., M.C. in support to "X" Coy., and "Y" Coy. under command of 2/Lt. M.F. O'Donnell, M.C. in support to "W" Coy. Before starting a young subaltern from the Machine Gun Corps reported to me for duty. He had with him four guns, and I cannot remember the number of rank and file. His orders were to remain with me, and give me all the assistance at his disposal. The Royal Fusiliers were in support and the Lancashire Fusiliers in reserve. The leading Company "W" Coy. were rather sticky - being harassed heavily by machine gun fire from the Bosch. My Company "Y" reinforced him and after a short while we dislodged two heavy machine gun teams from near our objective, who caused the Battalion many casualties. We got very little support, I am sorry to say, from the machine gun company. I could neither find the officer nor his men during the advance. The Companies on the left did very well, and we got our objective shortly before dusk and harassed the enemy during his retreat. The Battalion suffered heavily. Major Rigg who commanded the Battalion was wounded, and several of the rank and file were wounded. "Y" Company's strength then numbered three officers (including myself) and fifty-six other ranks.

The Battalion was now commanded by Captain Oulton, M.C. who had shortly come out from home. Messages were received by Company Commanders at about 2.30 a.m. to report at Battalion headquarters. This we did, and were ordered to withdraw our men from the front line and take up our position in the assembly point in front of Krote where the Royal Fusiliers were billeted. We had to be in the assembly position by 7.30 a.m. The withdrawal was apparently made on account of the Divisions being held up on our left and right. Our orders were that a Barrage would go down - not before eight o'clock a.m. and we were to advance in the reverse order of the previous day, i.e. Z and Y Coys. leading, X and W in support. The Royal Fusiliers were to support us. On reaching a certain point on the map - about 800 yards in front of the villages of St. Louis and Krote, we were to turn south and form a defensive flank. I should have mentioned that our withdrawal was only for a distance of about three hundred yards. No barrage went down before three o'clock p.m. and meanwhile the battalion was being heavily shelled. Refugees were wending their way back towards our lines all day. Just as our barrage went down, Lt. O'Donnell was severely wounded - shoulder and left thigh and other parts of the body. He sent for Lt. Scott and handed over command of his Company to this subaltern. The Company then comprised two subalterns and fifty-four other ranks.